JAGUAR
SUPER SPORTS
FIXED HEAD COUPE

3½ LITRE XK 120 MODELS

OPERATING, MAINTENANCE AND SERVICE HANDBOOK

PRICE **5/-**

CHASSIS NUMBERS

| Super Sports | .. | 660001 Right-Hand Drive. | 670001 Left-Hand Drive. |
| Fixed Head Coupe.. | | 669001 Right-Hand Drive. | 679001 Left-Hand Drive. |

ENGINE NUMBERS
W.1001 onwards.
Suffix /7 or /8 of Engine Number denotes Compression Ratio.

JAGUAR CARS LIMITED, COVENTRY, ENGLAND

Telephone
88681 COVENTRY (Ten Lines)

Code : BENTLEY'S SECOND

Telegraphic Address
"JAGUAR," COVENTRY

Directors :
WILLIAM LYONS, Chairman and Managing Director
T. WELLS DAFFERN, O.B.E., F.C.A., F.S.A.A.

A. WHITTAKER, General Manager.   W. M. HEYNES, M.I.Mech.E. (A.D.), M.S.A.E.

INTRODUCTION

THIS handbook sets out the necessary details to ensure the satisfactory operation and maintenance of the Jaguar 3½ Litre XK 120.

Repairs and major service attentions are not described and the owner is recommended to have operations not covered by this book executed by the local Jaguar distributor or dealer, who is in a position to give authoritative advice and service.

The satisfactory running and fine performance of which the car is capable depends to a great extent upon the care and attention which it receives from the owner, and we earnestly recommend that careful attention be paid to the following instructions and the appropriate service be carried out at the suggested periods.

Every effort has been made to provide the essential information regarding the upkeep of the car as concisely as possible and in a manner which allows for rapid reference. To this end the handbook is divided into three parts; Part I deals with data, descriptions and operating instructions only; Part II which deals with maintenance gives first a summary of routine maintenance, a maintenance chart and recommended lubricants, this being followed by detailed maintenance of each component in alphabetical order enlarging on the summarised instructions; and Part III, Service Instructions which are considered might be of value to the enthusiast.

IMPORTANT

If it is necessary to communicate with the factory concerning this vehicle, it is essential to quote the Chassis Number. The appropriate number will be found stamped on a plate situated on the scuttle under the bonnet.

NOTE

Throughout this handbook reference to right hand and left hand is made assuming the driver to be seated in the car and facing forward.

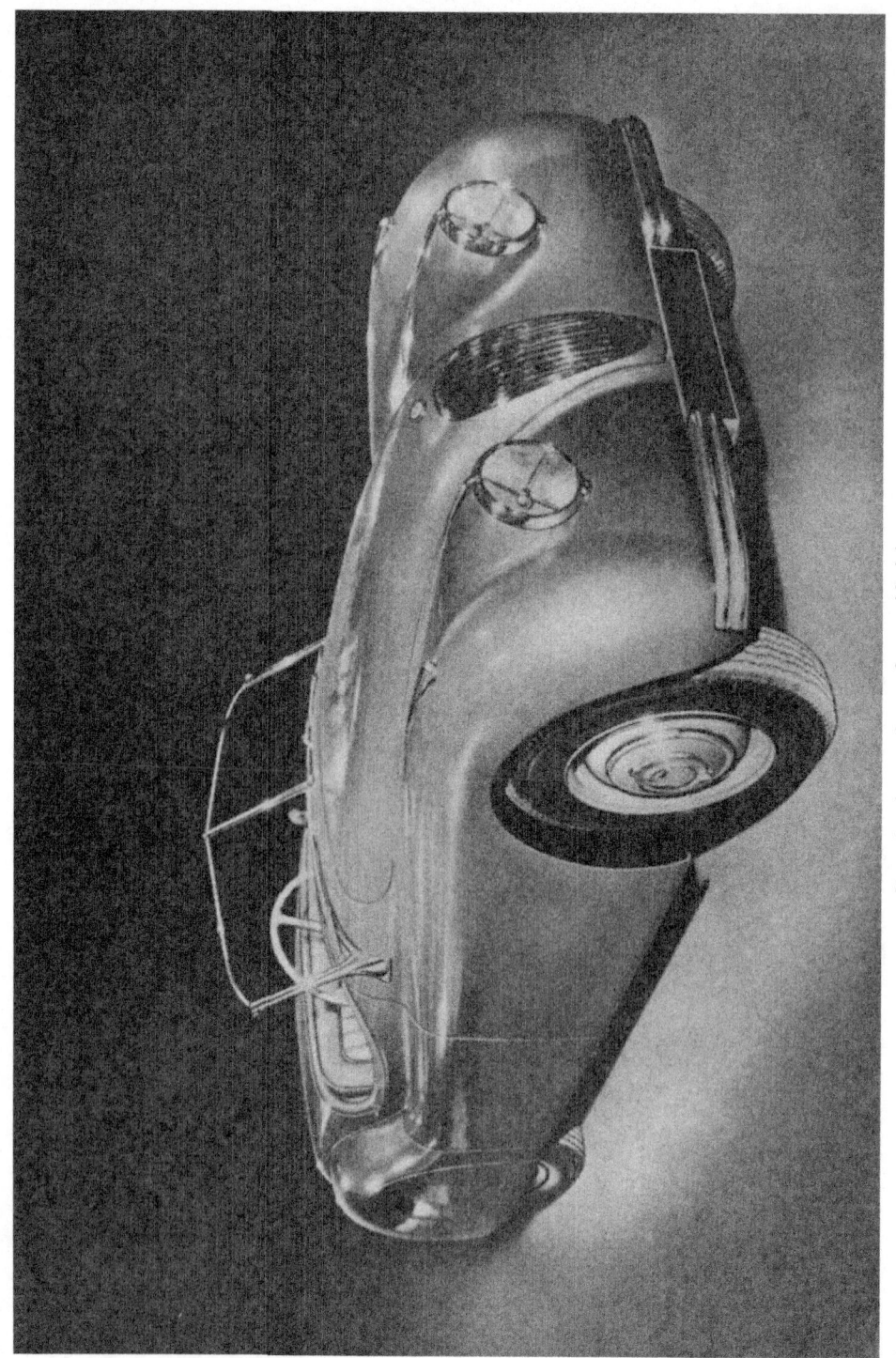

Plate 1. Jaguar Super Sports Model.

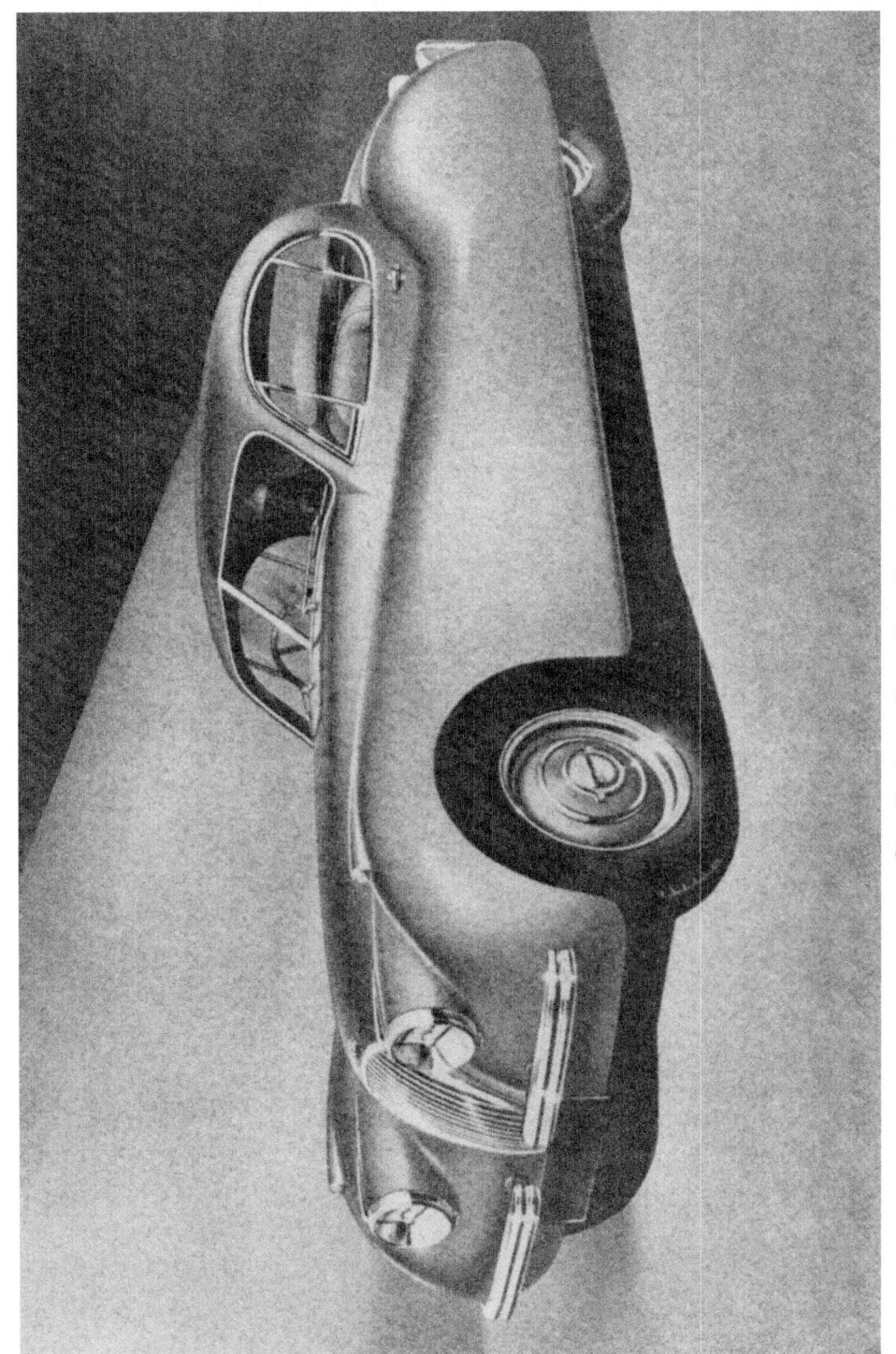

Plate 2. Jaguar Fixed Head Coupe Model.

INDEX TO CONTENTS

GENERAL

Accessories and Equipment Manufacturers	
Conversion Tables	
Guarantee	
Index to Contents	6
Index to Plates	9
Introduction	3
Service Departments	55

PART I. OPERATING INSTRUCTIONS

Accessories .. 20
- Brake Light
- Cigar Lighter
- Door Locks
- No-draught Ventilation
- Petrol Filler
- Rear Boot Light
- Reverse Light
- Scuttle Ventilators
- Seat Adjustment
- Steering Wheel Adjustment
- Tool Compartment
- Two-pin Socket

Air Conditioning Equipment	26
Frost Precautions	22
Hood—Raising, Lowering and Stowing	25
Instruments and Controls	15

- Foot Controls
- Hand Controls
- Instruments

Memoranda	11
Performance Data	14
Specification	12

- Air Conditioning Installation
- Brakes
- Chassis Frame
- Coachwork
- Electrical
- Engine
- Fuel Supply
- Gear Ratios
- Hood
- Instruments
- Jacking
- Seating
- Steering
- Suspension
- Transmission
- Wheels and Tyres

Starting and Driving	21

- Starting
- Driving

Running-in Instructions	21
Wheel Changing	23

PART II. MAINTENANCE INSTRUCTIONS

Recommended Lubricants	29
Fill up Data	29
Tyre Pressures	29
Maintenance Chart	30
Summary of Maintenance	31

INDEX TO CONTENTS—*continued.*

Detailed Maintenance

Air Cleaners	36
Battery	32
Brakes. Adjustment General	32
,, Fronts	32
,, Rears	32
,, Hand	33
Hydraulic System	33
Carburetter and Fuel Pump Filters	36
Carburetter Dash Pot Chambers	36
Clutch	33
Coachwork. Carpets	33
Cellulose	33
Chromium Plate	34
Hood	34
Interior Hide	34
Cooling System	34
Distributor	37
Electrical. Bulb Data	35
Head Lamps	34
Side Lamps	34
Number Plate Lamps	34
Rear Lamps	34
Fuses	35
Fan Bearings	37
Fan Belt	37
Front Suspension	38
Gearbox	38
Oil Can Lubrication	38
Oil Filter	37
Oil Sump	37
Propeller Shaft	39
Rear Axle	39
Rear Suspension	39
Sparking Plugs	37
Steering	40
Tyres	40
Water Pump	38
Wheel Bearings. Front	40
Rear	40

INDEX TO CONTENTS—*continued*.

PART III. SERVICE INSTRUCTIONS

Engine
	Page
Decarbonising and Grinding Valves..	43
Tune up Data ..	43
Valve Clearance Adjustment..	44
Tightening Torque Data	46
Carburetter Tuning ..	46
Engine, Clutch and Gearbox Removal	48
Sparking Plugs ..	49

Brakes
To Bleed System	48

Front Suspension
Front Shock Absorbers	48
Adjustment of Torsion Rods..	49
Camber Setting	50
Castor Setting ..	50

Hub Races
Adjustment and Servicing	51

Steering
Track Adjustment	52
Steering Lock Adjustment	52
Steering Unit Adjustment	52

Suspension Rubber Bushes
Servicing..	53

Windscreen
To Remove and Refit..	54

INDEX TO PLATES

PLATE	PLATE No.	PAGE
Jaguar Super Sports Model	1	4
Jaguar Fixed Head Coupe Model	2	5
Instruments. Super Sports Model	3	15
Instruments and Controls. Fixed Head Coupe Model	4	16
Controls. Super Sports Model	5	17
Bonnet Safety Catch	6	18
Gear Positions	7	19
Drain Tap. Radiator	8	22
Drain Tap. Engine	9	22
Rear Wing Valance	10	23
Road Wheel Fixing Nuts	11	23
Spare Wheel Stowage	12	24
Jacking	13	24
Hood Retaining Catches	14	25
Hood Stowed	15	25
Air Conditioner 'HOT-COLD' Control	16	26
Jaguar XK 120 Maintenance Chart	17	30
Nipple. Foot Brake Pedal	18	32
Nipple. Front Wheel Bearings	19	33
Adjustment. Rear Brakes	20	33
Fuses	21	36
Distributor	22	37
Fan Belt Adjustment	23	37
Oil Filter	24	38
Propeller Shaft	25	39
Rear Axle	26	39
Steering Box Filler Plug	27	40
Nipple. Rear Wheel Bearing	28	40
Nipples. Steering	29	41
Engine. Exploded View	30	42
Timing Chain Adjustment	31	46
Carburetters	32	47
Torsion Rod Adjustment	33	49
Castor and Camber Adjustments	34	51

NOTES

PART I. OPERATING INSTRUCTIONS

MEMORANDA

Chassis Number .. ..
(Stamped at front of left-hand chassis side member and three feet (·90 metres) to rear of this point.)

Engine Number .. ..
(Stamped on the right-hand side of the cylinder block above the pressure oil filter.)

Body Number .. ..
(Embossed on a small plate attached to the left-hand side of the scuttle under the bonnet.)

Gearbox Number .. ..
(Stamped on a small 'shoulder' at the top of the rear left-hand side of the gearbox casing and also on the rim of the core plug aperture in the top cover.)

All four numbers are given on a plate under the bonnet at the rear of the engine.

Date of Car Purchase .. ..

Registration Number .. ..

Number of Cylinders	6
Bore	3·2677" (83 mm.)
Stroke	4·1732" (106 mm.)
Cubic Capacity	3442 c.c. (210 cu. ins.)
R.A.C. Rating	25·6 h.p.
Wheel Base	8' 6" (2·591 metres)
Track, Front	4' 3" (1·295 metres)
" Rear	4' 2" (1·270 metres)
Super Sports—Length (Overall)	14' 5½" (4·406 metres)
Width	5' 2" (1·575 metres)
Height	4' 4½" (1·333 metres)
Fixed Head Coupe—Length (Overall)	14' 5½" (4·406 metres)
Width	5' 2" (1·575 metres)
Height	4' 5" (1·346 metres)
Turning Circle	31' (9·45 metres)
Ground Clearance	7⅛" (181 mm.)
Super Sports—Weight (Dry)	24·5 cwts. (1245 kgs.) (2744 lbs.)
Fixed Head Coupe—Weight (Dry)	25·5 cwts. (1295 kgs.) (2856 lbs.)

CAR RADIO (if fitted)

Maker's Number .. ..

Number of Valves .. ..

Weight .. ..

PART I. OPERATING INSTRUCTIONS

SPECIFICATION

ENGINE
General

Type	3½ Litre
	Twin Overhead Camshaft
Bore	3·2677" (83 mm.)
Stroke	4·1732" (106 mm.)
Number of Cylinders	6
Capacity	3442 c.c. (210 cu. ins.)
R.A.C. Rating	25·6 h.p.
Maximum B.H.P.	160 @ 5200 r.p.m.
Compression Ratio. Standard	7 : 1
High	8 : 1

The cylinder block and crankcase are an integral high grade iron casting with full length water jackets. The cylinder head is of high tensile aluminium alloy with spherical machined combustion chambers. Twin 70° overhead camshafts run in four bearings for each shaft. Aluminium alloy pistons with steel connecting rods. Thin steel shell connecting rod and main bearings. 2¾" diameter counterweighted crankshaft running in seven steel backed precision bearings. Forced feed lubrication throughout by submerged pump from floating suction filter. Tecalemit full flow oil cleaner. Twin horizontal S.U. carburetters incorporating auxiliary self-starting carburetter with automatic thermo-electric operation fitted with air cleaners. Timing gear driven by two stage duplex roller chains with automatic tensioning device and manual adjustment. S.U. electric pump draws petrol from a large capacity tank at the rear. (An extra capacity petrol tank is available to special order.) Cooling water is circulated by a centrifugal water pump, with by-pass water control, to a gallery alongside the block which ensures equal distribution between all cylinders. Provision is made on the left hand side of the cylinder block for the fitment of an American standard engine heater. (See frost precautions).

Transmission. Four-speed single helical gearbox with synchromesh on second, third and top. Ground teeth gears running on needle bearings. Centrally positioned gear lever with remote control. Single dry plate Borg & Beck 10" diameter clutch. Hardy Spicer propeller shaft with lubricating nipples fitted to needle bearing universal joints.

Rear axle hypoid spiral bevel three-quarter floating with offset pinion shaft.

Axle Ratios. 3·77 : 1 Standard ; 3·31 : High.

GEAR RATIOS

Top	1 : 1	Second	1·982 : 1
Third	1·367 : 1	First	3·375 : 1
	Reverse	3·375 : 1	

Steering. Burman recirculating ball worm and nut. Left or right-hand steering available. Steering wheel 17", adjustable for reach.

Brakes. Lockheed hydraulic brakes operating on all four wheels. Front brakes are the two leading shoe type, and are self adjusting. The rear brakes are the normal leading and trailing shoe type and are manually adjusted. 12" diameter alloy iron drums. Central fly-off hand brake operates mechanically on rear wheels only through entirely separate mechanism.

PART I. OPERATING INSTRUCTIONS

Wheels and Tyres. Pressed steel wheels with detachable chrome plated nave plates and five stud mounting for each wheel. Tyres, Dunlop Road Speed 6·00 x 16"; spare wheel carried in compartment at rear.

Chassis Frame. Straight plane steel box section frame of immense strength; torsional rigidity ensured by large box section cross members.

Jacking. A central jack socket on each side of the car raises both wheels simultaneously with the minimum of effort by means of a special easy-lift jack.

Electrical Equipment. Lucas de Luxe throughout, 12 volt 64 amp. capacity, twin batteries with constant voltage controlled ventilated dynamo, 10 hour discharge, flush head lamps and wing lamps, stop light, reverse light, twin rear lights, panel light, twin blended-note horns, twin blade screen wiper, cigar lighter, starter motor, vacuum and centrifugal automatic ignition advance. Fixed Head Coupe fitted with twin interior lights and flasher indicators. Built-in provision for Radiomobile car radio on Fixed Head Coupe Model.

Suspension. Independent front suspension incorporating transverse wishbones and long torsion bars with telescopic type hydraulic shock absorbers. Rear suspension by long silico manganese steel half elliptic springs controlled by Girling PV.7 hydraulic shock absorbers.

Fuel Supply. By a large capacity S.U. electric pump from a 15 gallon rear tank, petrol filler cap concealed and fitted with lock and key.

Instruments. 5" diameter 140 m.p.h. speedometer, 5" diameter revolution counter, ammeter, oil pressure gauge, water thermometer gauge, petrol gauge with warning light, electric clock.

Coachwork—Super Sports Model. Aerodynamic two-seater body upholstered throughout in finest quality leather hides, floor is thickly carpeted over felt underlay. Instrument panel and garnish rails finished in first quality leather hide, capacious pockets in the doors. Ample accommodation is provided in a capacious rear locker, provided with an automatic light.

Seating. Divided seat and squab, folding forward for access to hood and battery, seats adjustable for reach. A tonneau cover is provided.

Hood. Finest quality mohair material, concealed behind seats when folded fitted with unbreakable rear light. Detachable side screens stored in tray in the hood compartment.

Coachwork—Fixed Head Coupe. Aerodynamic two-seater body upholstered throughout in finest quality Vaumol leather hide. Floor thickly carpeted over felt underlay. Instrument panel and garnish rails are of fine quality figured walnut. Cubby locker on passenger side of instrument panel. Ventilator windows at front of door lights and in rear quarters. Ample luggage accommodation in rear locker provided with automatic light. Manually operated scuttle ventilators provide cool air in car when required.

Air Conditioning Installation. Provides recirculated air conditioning of body interior, demisting and defrosting of windscreen.

PART I. OPERATING INSTRUCTIONS

PERFORMANCE DATA

The following tables show the relationship between engine revolutions per minute to vehicle speed in miles per hour and kilometres per hour for the various gear ratios.

It is recommended that engine revolutions in excess of the following maximum should not be exceeded for long periods.

5000 r.p.m.

AXLE RATIO 3·77 : 1 (Standard)

Kilos per hour	Miles per hour	First and Reverse 12·72	Second 7·47	Third 5·15	Top 3·77	True r.p.m. in top, allowing for changes in tyre radius (Dunlop Road Speed 16 x 6.00) due to effect of centrifugal force. Tyres at 35 lbs. sq. in. (2.46 kg./cm^2).
16	10	1,579	928	639	468	
32	20	3,158	1,856	1,278	936	
48	30	4,737	2,784	1,917	1,404	
64	40		3,712	2,556	1,872	
80	50		4,640	3,195	2,340	2,323
96	60		5,568	3,834	2,808	2,774
112	70			4,473	3,276	3,217
128	80			5,112	3,744	3,651
144	90			5,751	4,212	4,075
160	100				4,680	4,488
176	110				5,148	4,890
192	120				5,616	5,279

AXLE RATIO 3·31 : 1 (High)

Kilos per hour	Miles per hour	First and Reverse 11·17	Second 6·56	Third 4·52	Top 3·31	True r.p.m. in top, allowing for changes in tyre radius (Dunlop Road Speed 16 x 6.00) due to effect of centrifugal force. Tyres at 35 lbs. sq. in. (2.46 kg./cm^2).
16	10	1,399	815	561	411	
32	20	2,798	1,630	1,122	822	
48	30	4,197	2,445	1,683	1,233	
64	40	5,596	3,260	2,244	1,644	1,638
80	50		4,075	2,805	2,055	2,039
96	60		4,890	3,366	2,466	2,434
112	70		5,705	3,927	2,877	2,822
128	80			4,488	3,288	3,203
144	90			5,049	3,699	3,575
160	100			5,610	4,110	3,938
176	110				4,521	4,291
192	120				4,932	4,633
208	130				5,343	4,963
224	140				5,754	5,282

PART I. OPERATING INSTRUCTIONS

INSTRUMENTS AND CONTROLS

INSTRUMENTS

(Refer to Plate 3, Super Sports, and Plate 4, Fixed Head Coupe.)

Ammeter. Records the flow of current into or out of the battery. Since compensated voltage control is incorporated the flow of current is adjusted to the state of charge of the battery ; thus when the battery is fully charged the dynamo provides only a small output and therefore little charge is registered on the ammeter, whereas when the battery is low a continuous high charge is shown.

Head Lamp Warning Light. A red warning light is situated in the speedometer and lights up when the head lamps are in the full beam position and is automatically extinguished when the lamps are in the dipped beam position.

Ignition Warning Light. A red warning light situated immediately below the lamp switch on the Super Sports Model and to the left of the light switch on the Fixed Head Coupe Model lights up and records 'IGN.' when the ignition is switched 'ON' and the engine is not running or when the engine is running at a speed insufficient to charge the battery. The latter circumstances are not harmful but always switch 'OFF' when the engine is not running.

Oil Pressure and Water Temperature Gauge. The oil pressure gauge records the oil pressure being delivered by the oil pump to the engine ; it does not record the quantity of oil in the sump. The minimum pressure at maintained high r.p.m. when hot should not be less than 40 lbs. per square inch. The water temperature gauge records the temperature of the coolant by means of a bulb screwed into the thermostat housing, which is connected to the gauge by a capillary tube.

Petrol and Oil Level Gauge. Records the quantity of petrol in the supply tank. Readings will only be obtained when the ignition is switched 'ON.' By pressing the oil level switch, situated at the lower right-hand side of the facia board, the gauge records the approximate quantity of oil in the engine sump.

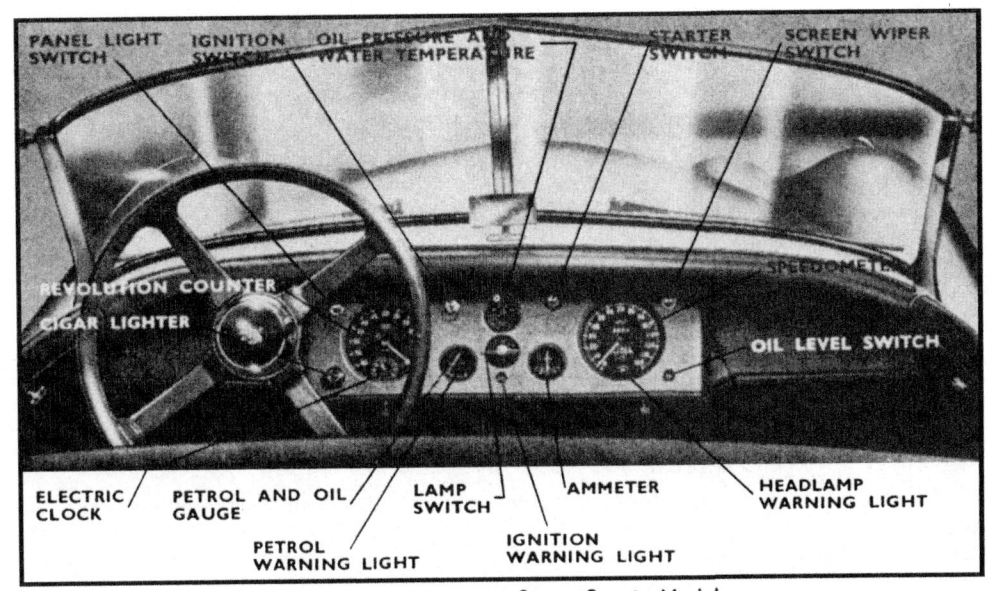

Plate 3. Instruments—Super Sports Model.

PART I. OPERATING INSTRUCTIONS

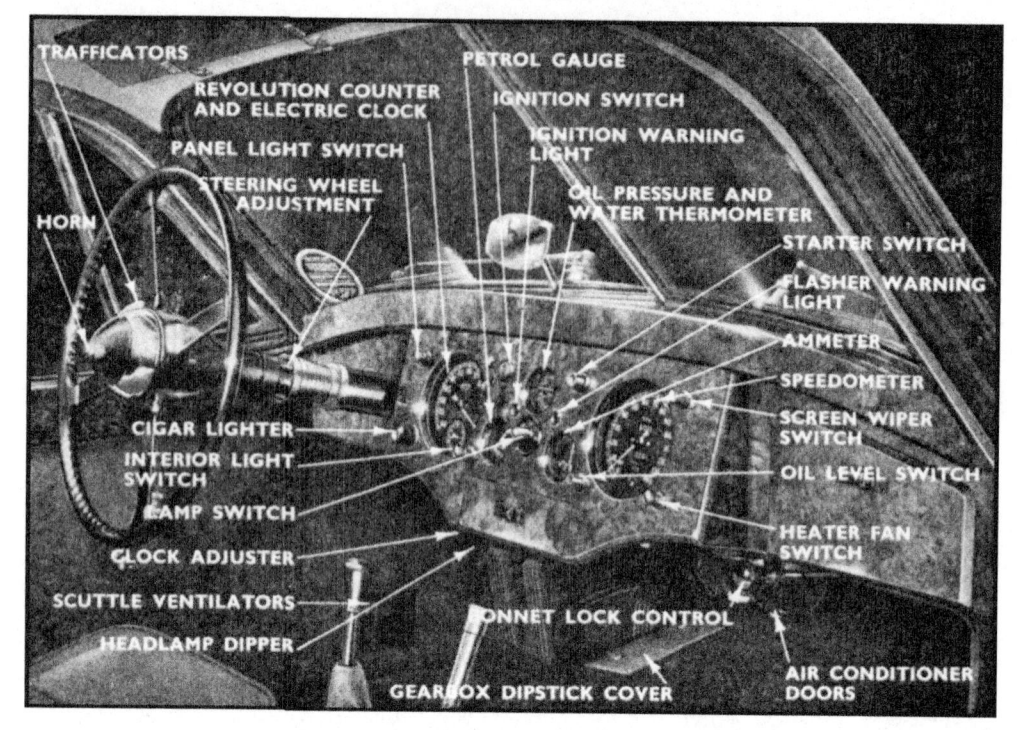

Plate 4. Instruments and Controls—Fixed Head Coupe Model.

Petrol Level Warning Light. A red light is situated in the petrol gauge and lights up intermittently when the petrol level in the tank becomes low. When the petrol is almost exhausted the warning lamp operates continuously.

Revolution Counter and Clock. Records the speed of the engine in revolutions per minute. The built-in electric clock is powered by the battery. The clock hands may be adjusted by pushing up the stem winder and rotating clockwise. Starting is accomplished in the same manner.

Speedometer. Records the vehicle speed in miles per hour, total mileage and trip mileage. (Kilometres on certain export models.) The trip figures may be set to zero by pushing the knob under the facia upwards and rotating anti-clockwise.

Trafficator Warning Light—Fixed Head Coupe. An amber light, situated to the right of the lamp switch, lights up and records 'TRF' when the trafficators are in use. Trafficators only operate when the ignition is switched ' ON.'

FOOT CONTROLS

(Refer to Plate 5, Super Sports, and Plate 4, Fixed Head Coupe Model.)

Accelerator. The pedal on the right. Controls the speed of the engine.

Brake. The centre pedal. Operates the brakes on all four wheels.

Clutch. The pedal on the left. Connects and disconnects the engine and the transmission. Never drive with a foot resting on the pedal and do not keep the pedal depressed for long periods in traffic. Never coast the car with gear engaged and clutch depressed.

PART I. OPERATING INSTRUCTIONS

Head Lamp Dipper. Situated on the toe boards and operated by foot. The switch is of the change over type and if the head lamps are in the full beam position a single pressure on the control will switch the lamps to the dipped beam position and they will remain so until another single pressure switches them to the full beam position again.

Plate 5. Controls—Super Sports Model.

PART I. OPERATING INSTRUCTIONS

HAND CONTROLS

(Refer to Plate 5, Super Sports, and Plate 4, Fixed Head Coupe Model.)

Air Conditioner Equipment Controls. On the Fixed Head Coupe the rheostat switch for the air conditioner motor is situated at the lower extreme right-hand side of the facia panel. On the Super Sports the switch is situated on the facia panel forward of the steering wheel.

The motor switch knob is off when rotated fully anti-clockwise. Rotation clockwise switches on the motor at its maximum speed, further rotation clockwise brings the rheostat into operation and the motor speed progressively falls until the knob reaches the end of its travel.

Observe that the motor switch is wired through the ignition switch and will be automatically switched off with the ignition.

The control knob for the hot water supply to the air conditioner unit is situated on the scuttle to the rear of the engine and is accessible when the bonnet is raised. Rotate knob clockwise for cold and anti-clockwise for hot. For full instructions on use of air conditioner equipment see page 26.

Plate 6. Bonnet Safety Catch.

PART I. OPERATING INSTRUCTIONS

Bonnet Lock Control. The bonnet lock is controlled from the driving compartment. To open the bonnet pull the control knob, situated at the right-hand under the facia. This will release the bonnet which will now be retained by the safety catch. Insert the fingers under the nose of the bonnet and pull the safety catch, which is attached to the bonnet, forward when the bonnet may be raised and retained in the open position by the support strut. The bonnet is self-locking when pushed down firmly into the closed position.

Gear Lever. Centrally situated and with gear positions indicated on the control knob. Always engage neutral and release the clutch when the car is at rest.

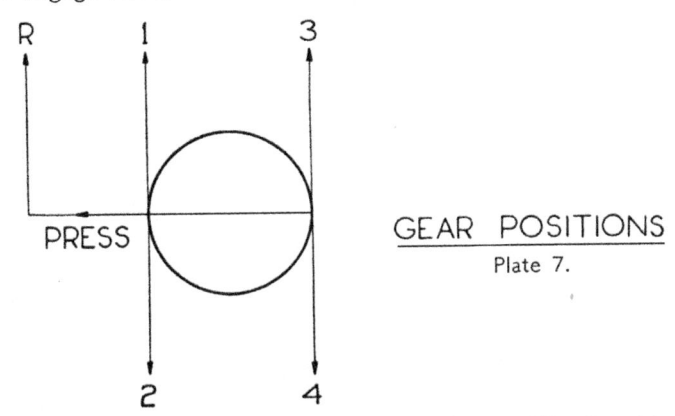

GEAR POSITIONS
Plate 7.

Hand Brake Lever. Positioned beside the gear lever. The hand brake operates mechanically on the rear wheels only and is provided for parking, driving away on a hill and when at a standstill in traffic. To apply the brake, pull the lever back and press down the thimble when the ratchet will engage. The hand brake is released by pulling back the lever when it will fly off.

Horn Switch. Situated in the centre of the steering wheel it operates the twin horns when depressed.

Ignition Switch. The key provided operates the switch, when inserted and turned clockwise.

Never leave the ignition switched on when the engine has stopped, a reminder of such circumstances is provided by the ignition warning light which will then light up and record ' IGN.'

Interior Light Switch—Fixed Head Coupe Model. Operate the switch to illuminate the car interior by the twin lights fitted in the rear quarters.

Lamp Switch. From 'OFF' can be rotated clockwise into two positions, giving in the first location side and tail, and in the second location head, side and tail.

Oil Level Switch. Operation of the switch obtains a reading on the petrol and oil level gauge indicating the quantity of oil in the engine sump. A true reading will only be obtained when the car is standing at rest on level ground. A positive check on the readings shown on the gauge may be obtained with the dip stick fitted to the left-hand rear of the cylinder block.

Panel Light Switch. Operate the switch when it is desired to read the instruments in darkness. The panel lights only operate when the side lamps are switched on.

Starter Switch. Press the switch, with the ignition switched on, to start the engine. Release the switch immediately the engine fires and never operate the starter when the engine is running. The starter only operates when the ignition is switched on.

PART I.   OPERATING INSTRUCTIONS

Trafficators. Operated by the knob situated at the top of the steering wheel centre. Normally the trafficators are self-cancelling when the wheel is centralised after turning a corner. When only a slight turn is made it may be necessary to cancel the trafficators manually by returning the control knob to the central position. When in use the warning lamp on the facia lights up intermittently and records ' TRF.' Operation of the trafficator switch causes bulbs in the side and stop lamps on the side selected to flash intermittently. (Fixed Head Coupe only).

Windscreen Wipers. The wipers are set in motion and parked following use by operation of the switch. Do not endeavour to move the wiper blades across the windscreen by hand.

ACCESSORIES

Brake Lights. Twin combined tail and brake lights are provided situated in the rear wings. The latter automatically light up when the foot brake is applied.

Cigar Lighter. Fitted to the facia board. Thermostatically controlled. To operate press holder into socket and remove hand. Holder will return to extended position in socket on reaching required temperature. Do not hold lighter in 'pressed in' position.

Door Locks—Super Sports Model. To open the door pull upwards the leather cable situated inside the doors. Doors may be locked by rotating the interior door locking catches and then closing doors.

Door Locks—Fixed Head Coupe Model. Doors may be opened from outside by rotating the exterior door handles. From inside by rotating the interior door handles. Both doors may be locked by rotating the ignition key in the locking barrel of the exterior door handles.

Petrol Filler. The petrol filler is situated in a recess above the left-hand rear wing, and is provided with a cover. This cover is unlocked with the key provided.

Reverse Light. The reverse light is automatically brought into operation when reverse gear is engaged and the side lights are switched on.

Rear Boot Light. The rear boot is automatically illuminated by a lamp in the lid when opened with the side lights switched on.

Seat Adjustment. Both seats are adjustable for reach. Push the lock bar, situated beside the inside runner towards the outside of the car and slide into the required position. Release the lock bar and slide until the mechanism engages with a click.

Scuttle Ventilators. Additional cool fresh air ventilation of the car interior may be obtained by opening one or both scuttle ventilators by operating the levers which protrude from the ventilator apertures on the inside of the scuttle side casings.

Steering Wheel Adjustment. Rotate the knurled ring at the base of the steering wheel hub in a clockwise direction when the steering wheel may be slid into the desired position. Tighten up the knurled ring to lock the steering wheel.

No Draught Ventilation—Fixed Head Coupe. No draught ventilator windows, incorporating quick locking catches, are fitted to the front end of the door lights and to the rear quarters.

Tool Compartment. The tools are carried in a container on the left-hand side of the rear boot. The jack, wheel brace and jack ratchet handle are stowed in the spare wheel compartment. Grease gun stowed in clips under bonnet. Tool roll stowed in boot compartment forward of petrol filler cowling.

PART I.   OPERATING INSTRUCTIONS

STARTING AND DRIVING

STARTING

(a)   Before starting the engine the new owner should be familiar with the location and function of the instruments and controls see (page 15).

(b)   Ensure that the water level in the radiator and the oil level in the sump are correct. Check for sufficient petrol in the tanks.

(c)   Place the gear lever in the neutral position and check that the hand brake is applied. Switch on the ignition and press the starter. Release the starter as soon as the engine fires—this is important.

(d)   It is not necessary to use any manual choke control when starting from cold, since the auxiliary starting carburetter is entirely automatic and controls the mixture strength without assistance from the driver. The starting carburetter automatically cuts out when the temperature of the water in the cylinder head reaches 35° C.

(e)   Do not operate the engine at high r.p.m. when first started, but allow time for the engine to warm up and the oil to circulate freely. A thermostat is fitted to assist in rapid warm up. In very cold weather run the engine at 1,500 r.p.m. with the car stationary until a rise in temperature is indicated on the temperature gauge.

DRIVING

(a)   Careful adherence to the instructions given in the next paragraph regarding "running in" will be amply repaid by obtaining the best performance and utmost satisfaction from the car.

(b)   The habit should be formed of reading the oil pressure gauge, water temperature gauge and ammeter occasionally as a check on the correct functioning of the car. Should an abnormal reading be obtained an investigation should be made immediately.

(c)   Always start from rest in first or second gear ; on a hill always use first gear. To start in a higher gear will cause excessive clutch slip and premature wear. Never drive with a foot resting on the clutch pedal and do not keep the clutch pedal depressed for long periods in traffic.

(d)   The synchromesh gearbox provides a synchronised change into second, third and top. When changing gear the movement should be slow and deliberate.

When changing down a smoother gear change will be obtained if the accelerator is left depressed to provide the higher engine speed suitable to the lower gear. Always fully depress the clutch pedal when changing gear.

(e)   Gear changing may be slightly stiff on a new car but this will disappear as the gearbox becomes run in.

(f)   Always apply the foot brake progressively ; fierce and sudden application is bad for the car and tyres. The hand brake is for use when parking the car, when driving away on a hill and when at a standstill in traffic.

RUNNING-IN INSTRUCTIONS

Only if the following important recommendations are observed will the high performance and continued good running of which the Jaguar is capable be obtained.

Throttle Restrictor. To prevent cars being run at an excessive speed during their early life it has been considered advisable to restrict the throttle opening by the fitting of a stop on the underside of the accelerator pedal. This stop is secured to the pedal by a setscrew which is in turn locked by a wire and lead seal.

PART I. OPERATING INSTRUCTIONS

The stop is to be removed at the time the free service is carried out, that is, after the first 500 miles (800 kilometres). During the time the car is run with the throttle restrictor fitted do not over-stress the engine. Use the gears so that the engine runs under light load with the minimum of throttle opening.

After 500 miles (800 kilometres) and up to 1,000 miles (1,500 kilometres) do not exceed 2,500 r.p.m. and from 1,000 miles to 2,000 miles (3,000 kilometres) do not exceed 3,000 r.p.m. Continue to drive without over-stressing the engine. Have the engine sump drained and refilled and the oil filter attended to as recommended at the free service, that is, after the first 500 miles (800 kilometres).

FROST PRECAUTIONS

(Refer to Plates 8 and 9.)

During the winter months it is recommended that an approved anti-freeze solution should be added to the cooling water in the proportions recommended by the appropriate manufacturer.

If an anti-freeze solution is not used it is essential to adhere closely to the following instructions, otherwise it is likely that severe and expensive damage will be caused to the engine. Drain the radiator while the car is standing on level ground by opening the drain tap situated at the front of the radiator block, and the engine by opening the tap at the left-hand rear of the cylinder block.

When water has ceased to flow, run the engine at 1,000 r.p.m. for 30 seconds to dry out any remaining water pockets. Observe that it is essential to open both drain taps to drain the cooling system completely.

NOTE.—On cars fitted with air conditioners note that draining the radiator and cylinder block does NOT drain the heater unit.

Engine Heater. Provision is made on the left hand side of the cylinder block slightly forward of the engine dipstick, for the fitment of an American standard engine heater element No. 7 manufactured by "The Electrical Heating & Manufacturing Company".

Plate 8.
Drain Tap—Radiator.

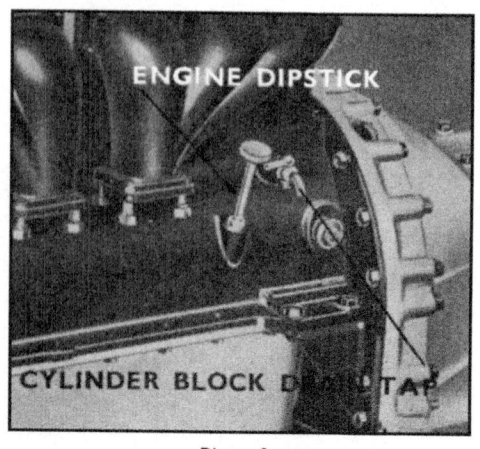

Plate 9.
Drain Tap—Engine.

PART I. OPERATING INSTRUCTIONS

WHEEL CHANGING (Refer to Plates 10, 11, 12 and 13.)

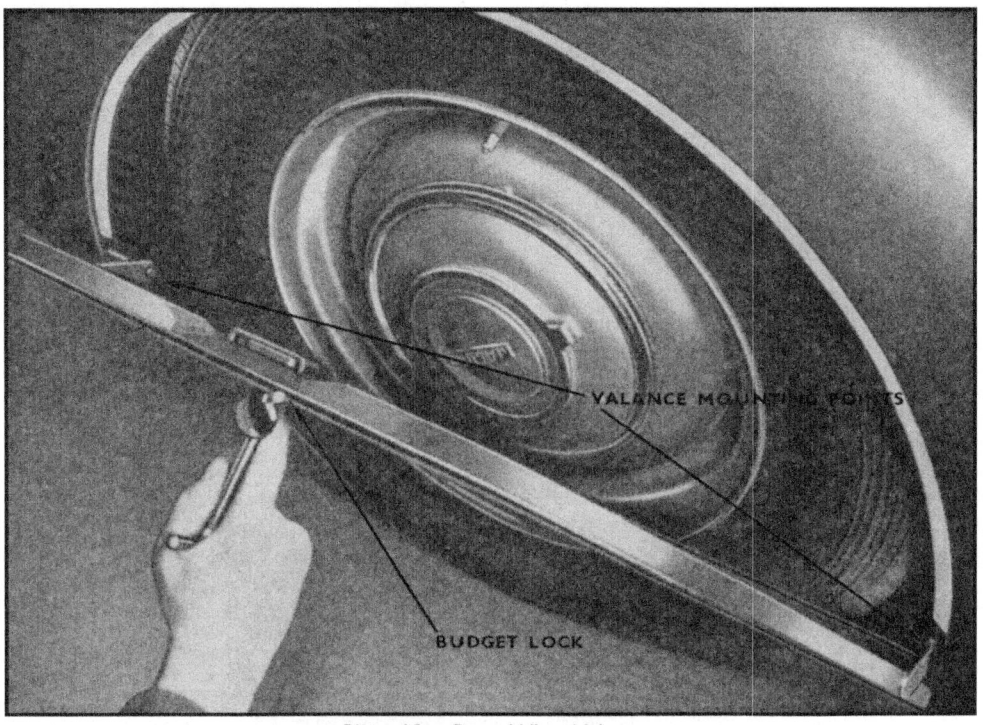

Plate 10. Rear Wing Valance.

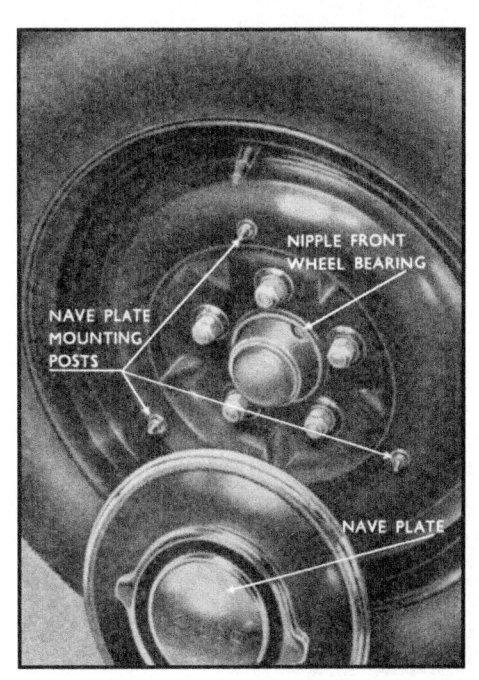

Whenever possible wheel changing should be carried out with the car standing on level ground and in all cases with the hand brake fully applied.

Remove the jack, jack ratchet handle, wheel brace and 'T' key which are housed together with the spare wheel in the spare wheel compartment. Using the wheel brace release the spare wheel retaining screw by rotating the nut anti-clockwise, withdraw the spare wheel to the rear.

Remove the rear wing valance if a rear wheel is to be changed, by inserting the 'T' key in the chrome plated budget lock and rotate a quarter of a turn. Draw the top of the valance outwards and lift upwards and out of engagement from the mounting points. Remove the road wheel nave plate by levering this off with the screwdriver blade formed at the handle end of the wheel brace.

Plate 11. Road Wheel Fixing Nuts.

PART I.   OPERATING INSTRUCTIONS

Using the wheel brace loosen, but do not remove, the five road wheel fixing nuts. Observe that all wheel nuts have right-hand threads, that is, they are removed by anti-clockwise rotation of the wheel brace. Open the door on the side of the car to be raised and slide the carpet from under the chromium plated strip at the base of the door shut. Remove the cover plate now disclosed by lifting the spring-loaded handle upwards. Insert the square portion of the jack well home in the chassis frame jack socket situated under the floor and raise the side of the car by elevating the jack with the ratchet handle, fitted side marked 'LIFT' upwards, until the wheels are clear of the ground. Remove the wheel nuts and withdraw the road wheel.

Plate 12.   Spare Wheel Stowage.

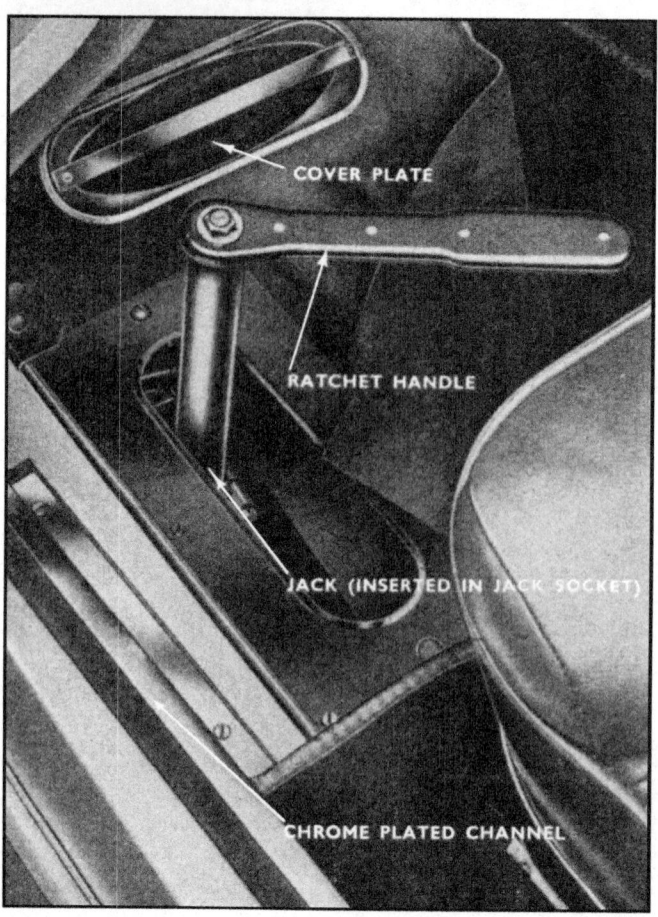

Plate 13. Jacking.

PART I. OPERATING INSTRUCTIONS

Mount the spare wheel on the fixing studs and start all five nuts on the threads by rotating clockwise. Apply the wheel brace and run all nuts up until they are tight. Lower the jack, using the jack ratchet handle side marked 'LOWER' upwards, until the weight of the car is on the wheels and finally tighten all wheel nuts.

Fit the nave plate over two of the three mounting posts and secure by a sharp tap from the hand at a point in line with the third mounting post. Refit the rear wing valance if this has been removed. Fit the spare wheel in the compartment and stow the tools.

RAISING AND STOWING THE HOOD

(Refer to Plates 14 and 15.)

Raising. Remove the tonneau cover, if fitted. Pull the seat back rests forward to disclose the hood stowed in the recess behind. Lift out the hood and open hood frame to the up position. Engage rear of hood in slide-in brackets in rear panel. Return seat backs to normal position and sit in car. Engage channel rail at front of hood over top of screen frame, engage and lock the two outer hood fixing clips simultaneously. Then engage and lock centre fixing clip. Finally secure hood to body sides at rear of doors by press studs.

Plate 14.
Hood Retaining Catches.

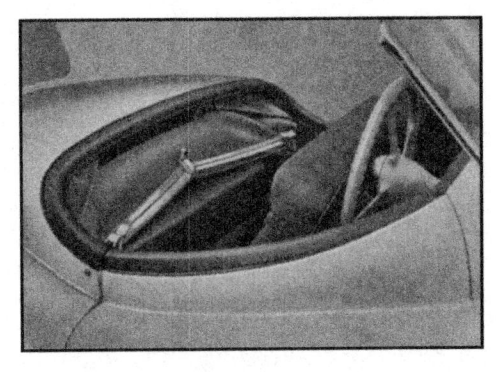

Plate 15.
Hood Stowed.

Stowing. Remove and stow the side curtains. Pull the seat back rests forward. Collapse the hood frame, holding the hood fabric upwards to prevent it being trapped by the hood sticks. Turn the two outer sides of the hood fabric inside out over the main hood panel. Stow the rear portion of the hood containing the rear light, fold the hood frame fully down, then fold the hood fabric on top of the stowed hood frame. Return the seat backs to the normal position.

PART I. OPERATING INSTRUCTIONS

AIR CONDITIONING EQUIPMENT

Description. The air conditioning unit, consisting of heating element, fan and electric motor, is mounted on the scuttle under the facia immediately above the gearbox cowl. Engine cooling water may be circulated through the heating element by the water pump and an 'ON-OFF' tap. An 'ON-OFF' switch for the electric motor is also controlled by the driver. Suitable pipes deliver air from the air conditioning unit to vents at the base of the screen to provide demisting and defrosting of the screen. Situated on the face of the air conditioning unit are two doors which control the flow of air into the body of the car.

Controls. The 'HOT-COLD' control knob controlling the flow of water from the engine cooling system to the element is fitted on the scuttle at the rear of the engine and is accessible when the bonnet is raised. (See Plate 16.) The 'HOT-COLD' tap is set to hot when rotated fully anti-clockwise. Rotation fully clockwise sets the tap to cold. The tap will normally be left in the 'ON' or 'HOT' position during winter running and the 'OFF' or 'COLD' position during summer running.

On the Fixed Head Coupe the 'ON-OFF' rheostat switch for the air conditioner motor is situated at the lower extreme right-hand side of the facia panel. On the Super Sports the switch is situated on the facia panel, forward of the steering wheel.

The motor switch knob is off when rotated fully anti-clockwise. Rotation clockwise switches on the motor at its maximum speed, further rotation clockwise brings the rheostat into operation and the motor speed progressively falls until the knob reaches the end of its travel.

Observe that the motor switch is wired through the ignition switch and will be automatically switched off with the ignition.

DO NOT USE FORCE WHEN TURNING CONTROLS

Plate 16. Air Conditioner Hot/Cold Control.

PART I. OPERATING INSTRUCTIONS

OPERATING INSTRUCTIONS.

Unit not in use. (Air conditioning, demisting or defrosting not required.)
(a) Set motor to 'OFF.' (b) Close air conditioner doors.

Unit in use. Cold Air. (Demisting only.)
(a) Set motor to 'ON.' (b) Turn 'HOT-COLD' tap to 'COLD.' (c) Close air conditioner doors.

(Cold (recirculated) air conditioning and demisting.)
(a) Set motor to 'ON.' (b) Turn 'HOT-COLD' tap to 'COLD.' (c) Open air conditioner doors.

Unit in use. Warm Air. (Demisting and defrosting only.)
(a) Set motor to 'ON.' (b) Turn 'HOT-COLD' tap to 'HOT.' (c) Close the air conditioner doors.

(Warm (recirculated) air conditioning, demisting and defrosting.)
(a) Set motor to 'ON.' (b) Turn 'HOT-COLD.' tap to 'HOT.' (c) Open air conditioner doors.

Use the rheostat switch to control the speed of the fan.

PART II. MAINTENANCE INSTRUCTIONS

RECOMMENDED LUBRICANTS

Component	Vacuum	Wakefield	Shell	Essolube	Price's	S.A.E. Viscosity
Engine { Summer 32°F.-90°F.	Mobiloil A	Castrol X.L.	Double Shell	Essolube 30	Energol 30	30
Winter Below 32°F.	Mobiloil Arctic	Castrolite	Single Shell	Essolube 20	Energol 20	20
Tropical Above 90°F.	Mobiloil B.B.	Castrol X.X.L.	Triple Shell	Essolube 40	Energol 40	40
Gearbox / Carburetter Hydraulic Piston Dampers / Distributor / Oil Can Lubrication	Mobiloil A	Castrol X.L.	Double Shell	Essolube 30	Energol 30	30
Rear Axle	Mobilube G.X. 90	Castrol Hypoy.	Spirax 90 E.P.	Expee Compound 90	Energol Hypoid 90	Hypoid 90
Steering Gear / Steering Idle Lever Housing / Propeller Shaft Needle Bearings	Mobilube C	Castrol D	Spirax 140 E.P.	Gear Oil 140 (Heavy)	Energol 140	140
Water Pump / Fan / Propeller Shaft Spline / All Chassis Nipples / Wheel Bearings	Mobilgrease No. 5	Castrolease WB.	Retinax A	Esso High Temp. Grease	Belmoline H.M.P.	
Upper Cylinder Lubrication	Mobil Upperlube	Castrollo	Donax U.	Essomix	Energol U.C.L.	

Brake Supply Tank. Use only genuine Lockheed Orange Hydraulic Brake Fluid.
Rear Shock Absorbers. Use only Girling Piston Type Thin Oil.

FILL UP DATA

	British Imperial	U.S.	Litres
Engine, sump capacity	21 pints	25 pints	12 litres
Engine, total capacity	24 pints	28 pints	13·5 litres
Gearbox	2¼ pints	3 pints	1·4 litres
Rear Axle	3 pints	3½ pints	1·7 litres
Cooling System	25½ pints	29·8 pints	14·5 litres
Petrol Tank	15 gallons	17·5 gallons	68 litres

TYRE PRESSURES

Front
25 lbs. per sq. in., Cold
(1·8 kg./cm.^{2})

Rear
25 lbs. per sq. in., Cold
(1·8 kg./cm.^{2})

For fast driving when comfort is not of primary importance use 35 lbs. per sq. in., Front, and 35 lbs. per sq. in., Rear, Cold (2·5 kg./cm.^{2}).

PART II.   MAINTENANCE INSTRUCTIONS

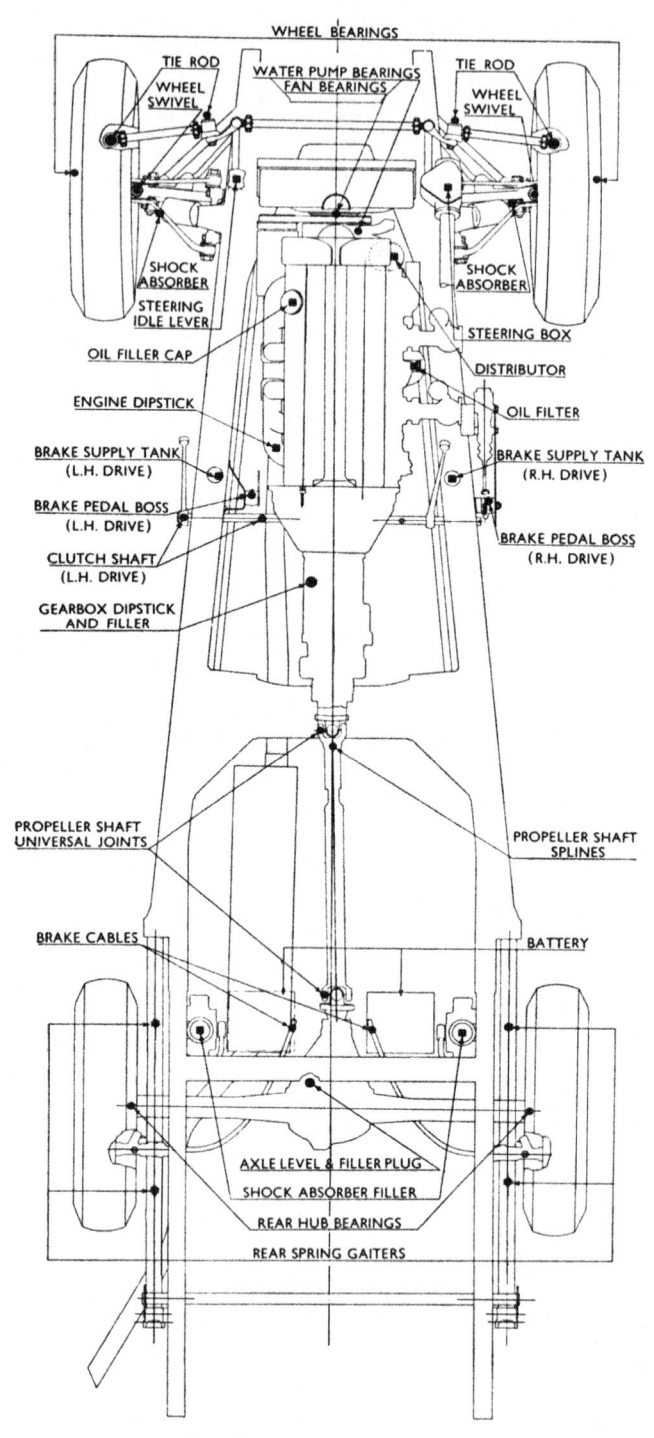

Plate 17.   Jaguar XK 120 Maintenance Chart.

PART II. MAINTENANCE INSTRUCTIONS

SUMMARY OF MAINTENANCE

(a) After the first 500 miles (800 kilometres) have the free service carried out. See Service Voucher issued with car.

DAILY. Check engine oil level, check radiator water level.

WEEKLY. Check tyre pressures.

(b) Every month or at 2,500 miles (4,000 kilometres).
1. Check and top up battery.
2. Drain and refill sump. Clean oil filter element.
3. Top up steering box, idle lever housing, gearbox and rear axle.
4. Lubricate all nipples (excluding hubs).
5. Lubricate carburetter dash pot chambers.
6. Lubricate distributor and adjust contact points.
7. Check and reset carburetter slow running.
8. Check and top up brake hydraulic supply tank.
9. Adjust rear brakes.
10. Check and adjust clutch pedal free travel.
11. Change over road wheels diagonally from front to rear.

(c) Every 5,000 miles (8,000 kilometres).
1. Carry out 2,500 miles service (b).
2. Clean, test and adjust sparking plugs.
3. Clean carburetter filter.
4. Lubricate all wheel bearing nipples.
5. Check and adjust fan belt.
6. Renew oil filter element.
7. Carry out oil can lubrication.
8. Wash air cleaner element/s.

(d) Every 10,000 miles (16,000 kilometres).
1. Carry out 2,500 miles service (b) and 5,000 miles service (c).
2. Drain and refill gearbox.
3. Drain and refill rear axle.
4. Check wheel bearings and adjust if necessary.
5. Clean out brakes and examine liners.
6. Clean and top up rear shock absorbers.
7. Clean fuel pump filter.
8. Check and tighten all chassis and body nuts, screws and bolts.

The number of grease nipples and their location is as follows:—

2 Nipples.	Steering tie rod (right hand).	2 Nipples.	Hand brake cables.
2 Nipples.	Steering tie rod (left hand).	4 Nipples.	Rear spring gaiters.
1 Nipple.	Wheel swivel (right hand).	2 Nipples.	Universal joints (propeller shaft).
1 Nipple.	Wheel swivel (left hand).		
1 Nipple.	Foot brake pedal boss.	1 Nipple.	Splines (propeller shaft).
1 Nipple.	Fan bearings.	4 Nipples.	Road wheel bearings.
1 Nipple.	Water pump bearing.		

PART II. MAINTENANCE INSTRUCTIONS

BATTERY

Every 2,500 miles (4,000 kilometres) examine the electrolyte level in the battery cells and top up, if necessary, using distilled water until the separators are just covered. Never use tap water, the impurities in which will be harmful to the battery. Clean the battery casing and ensure that all connections are clean and tight. The batteries are located immediately behind the front seats.

BRAKES

Every 2,500 miles (4,000 kilometres) examine the fluid level in the brake supply tank and, if necessary, top up with the recommended grade of fluid. Never allow the fluid level to fall more than 1" (25·0 mm.) from the top of the supply tank.

The tank is fitted on the left side of the dash on left-hand drive cars (Plate 21) and on the right side on right-hand drive.

Should it be found that the fluid level falls rapidly, indicating leakage from the system, the car should be immediately taken to the nearest Jaguar dealer for examination.

Every 2,500 miles (4,000 kilometres) lubricate the nipple on the foot brake pedal boss with the recommended grade of lubricant (Plate 18).

Every 2,500 miles (4,000 kilometres) lubricate the two nipples on the hand brake cables with the recommended grade of lubricant (Plate 26.)

These are accessible from underneath the car and are located on either side of the propeller shaft.

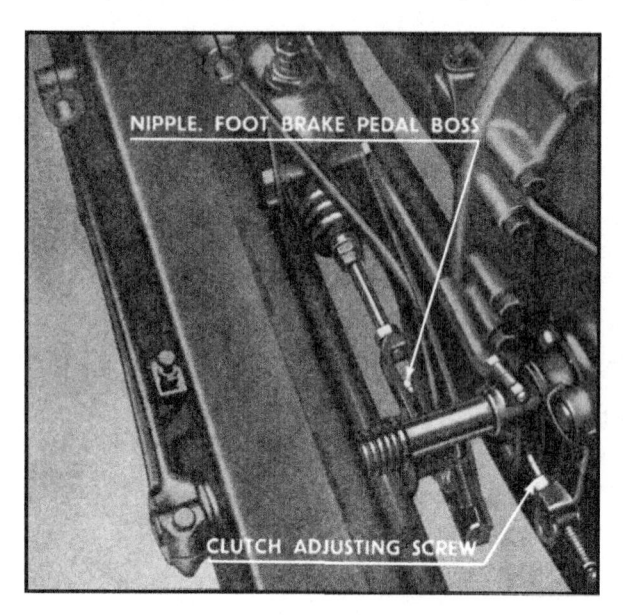

Plate 18. Nipple. Foot Brake Pedal.

Adjustment. The necessity for adjustment of the rear brakes cannot be laid down on a mileage or time basis, but can best be judged by observing the amount of brake pedal free travel before solid resistance is felt.

When this free travel is three quarters or more of the total available pedal pad travel, adjustment should be made as follows : (See Plate 20).

Fronts. The front wheel brakes are so designed that no manual adjustment for lining wear is necessary or provided for, as this automatically takes place when the foot brake is operated.

Rears. Place chocks under one front wheel and release the hand brake. Jack up one rear wheel until it is free to revolve. Remove the road wheel and rotate brake drum until the slotted adjusting screw can be seen through hole in outer face of drum. The position of the adjusting screw, is at front end of brake approximately 30° above the horizontal. Engage screw-driver blade with the slotted adjusting screw, turn the adjuster in an anti-clockwise direction until the brake shoe is in contact with the brake drum, then turn the adjuster back two clicks (clockwise) which should provide the correct clearance between the shoe and the drum. If closer adjustment is required spin the drum and apply the brakes hard. This will correctly position the shoe after which a further adjustment check should be made.

Repeat for the other rear wheel.

PART II.   MAINTENANCE INSTRUCTIONS

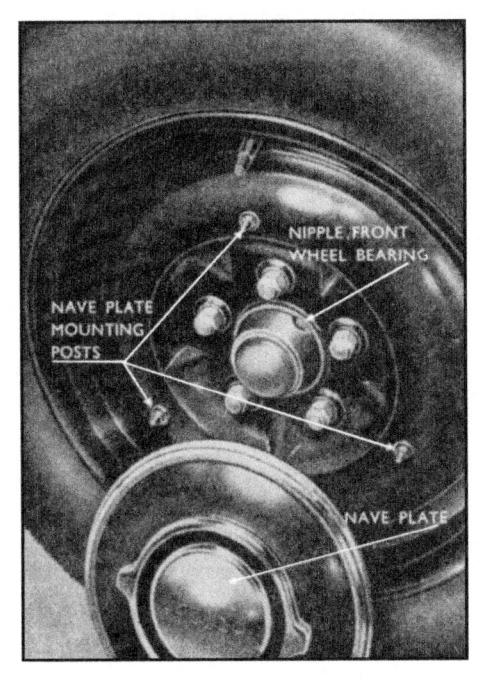

Plate 20.
Adjustment. Rear Brakes.
(L.H. rear brake illustrated.)

Plate 19. Nipple. Front Wheel Bearing.

Hand. Adjustment of the rear brakes will automatically adjust the hand brake, however it may be found that with the foot brake in correct adjustment excessive hand brake free travel is obtained. The hand brake has an individual adjustment situated in the operating cable immediately behind the centre cross member. Rotate the hexagon adjustment nut clockwise until the hand brake travels two notches on the ratchet before being fully applied, ensuring that no tension exists in the cables when the hand brake is in the 'off' position (Plate 25).

Hydraulic System. Should the resistance from the brake pedal become 'spongy' this indicates that air is present in the hydraulic system, possibly caused by the level of fluid in the supply tank having been allowed to fall too low.

In these circumstances it is necessary to 'bleed' the brakes, which consists of driving all air from the system, and it is recommended that this service be carried out by a Jaguar Dealer or Lockheed Service Depot.

Use only Lockheed Orange Hydraulic Brake Fluid, Girling Crimson Hydraulic Brake Fluid or Wagner 21 Hydraulic Brake Fluid, but on no account must the alternative brands of fluid be mixed in the system.

CLUTCH

Every 2,500 miles (4,000 kilometres) check the clutch free pedal travel and adjust if necessary. The correct adjustment is 1" (25 mm.) free or unloaded movement at the pedal pad. Adjustment is effected by an adjusting screw situated in the linkage. (Plate 18.)

COACHWORK

Carpets. These may be cleaned with petrol after the usual brushing.

Cellulose. Never clean the cellulose other than by washing with a soft sponge and hose pipe. Use a steady flow of water and sponge lightly. Dry and polish the cellulose with a good quality wash leather.

PART II. MAINTENANCE INSTRUCTIONS

Tar may be removed with a clean soft cloth moistened in petrol or with a proprietary brand of tar remover.

The cellulose may be polished from time to time with a good quality proprietary polish, either wax or emulsion type.

Chromium Plate. It is desirable to clean chromium plate occasionally to remove deposits which in time, if left undisturbed, will discolour the bright finish. It is, however, necessary to ensure that an abrasive cleaner is not employed as this will scratch and destroy the chrome.

Use an approved brand of chrome shine and apply this with a soft cloth.

Hoods. Care is necessary when cleaning not to destroy the waterproof qualities of the material. Cleaning may be carried out with a soft brush and a 'frothy' solution of soap and water.

Interior Hide. The seat upholstery may be kept clean by brisk rubbing with a wash leather well wrung out in water. Grease marks should be removed by light rubbing with a soft cloth moistened in petrol.

COOLING SYSTEM

Every day check the level of water in the radiator and top up, if necessary, to the bottom of the filler neck.

To preserve the efficiency of the cooling system it is desirable to use water which is as nearly neutral, that is, soft, as is procurable to fill and top up the system. Hard water produces scale which in time will affect the cooling efficiency of the system.

It is advantageous to flush out the system occasionally until the water runs clear.

ELECTRICAL

The replacement of bulbs is carried out as described in the following paragraphs.

Head Lamps. Remove fixing screw at base of rim, pull base of rim slightly forward and lift upwards and off. Release four securing screws, turn lamp anti-clockwise until heads of screws can be disengaged through the slotted holes in the flange and extract lamp. Disconnect wiring at bayonet socket and withdraw bulb carrier. The bulb can now be withdrawn from the carrier.

When replacing the light unit assembly, position it so that the heads of the adjusting screws protrude through the slotted holes in the flange. Press the unit in and turn in a clockwise direction being careful not to disturb the setting of the adjusting screws. When reassembling ensure that the four securing screws are retightened.

Refit the front rim, locating the top of the rim first and securing by means of the screw.

Head Lamp Focus. To raise head lamp beam rotate spring-loaded screw in top of lamp clockwise. To lower beam turn anti-clockwise.

To adjust head lamp beams to left or to right slacken the two hexagon headed screws, one at each side of the reflector rim assembly, and move the reflector assembly to the desired position.

Side Lamps. The rim and glass are retained in the side lamp shell by a small chrome screw. Remove the screw and withdraw the rim and glass complete.

Number Plate Lamps. These are situated above the rear number plate and incorporate the reverse light bulb. To gain access to the bulbs remove two chromium plated screws and withdraw the lamp covers.

Refitting is the reverse of the above procedure.

Rear Lamps. Situated in the rear wings the glass is mounted in a rubber grommet and retained by a chrome plated ring. Spring the ring out of the lip of the grommet and withdraw the glass.

PART II. MAINTENANCE INSTRUCTIONS

BULB DATA

Lamp	Lucas Bulb No.	Volts	Watts	Application
Head. Left-hand	302	12	48/48	Home.
Right-hand	185	12	48	
	303	12	48/48	Left-hand drive. Export.
	302	12	48/48	Right-hand drive. Export.
	Sealed Beam Unit			U.S.A. and Canada.
Side	989	12	6	
Side/Flasher	361	12	6/18	Fixed Head Coupe.
Number Plate	989	12	6	
Reverse	199	12	24	
Rear and Brake	361	12	6/18	
Rear and Brake/Flasher	361	12	6/18	Fixed Head Coupe.
Panel	207	12	6	
Rear Boot	256	12	3	
Interior Lights	256	12	3	Fixed Head Coupe.
Ignition, Head Lamp and Petrol Level Warning Lights.. ..	987	12	2·2	
Flasher Warning Light	987	12	2·2	Fixed Head Coupe.

Fuses. Should any component in the electrical system fail to function it is possible that the fuse protecting that component has blown. Should a replacement fuse of the correct type also blow, this indicates a fault in the circuit serving the affected component and the car should therefore be taken to the nearest Jaguar Dealer for examination.

Replacement of fuses is carried out at the control box situated on the left-hand side of the dash under the bonnet. The circuits served by the various fuses are as follows (Plate 21):—

'Aux.'   Interior lights (Fixed Head Coupe only).

PART II. MAINTENANCE INSTRUCTIONS

'Aux. Ign.'	Brake light ; petrol gauge ; windscreen wipers ; petrol warning light ; flasher lights and flasher unit ; horn relay ; air conditioner motor.
Fuse 1.	Cigar lighter.
Fuse 2.	Side and tail lights ; reverse light ; number plate light ; boot light.
Fuse 3.	Head lamp dipper.
Fuse 4.	Head lamps, head lamp warning light.

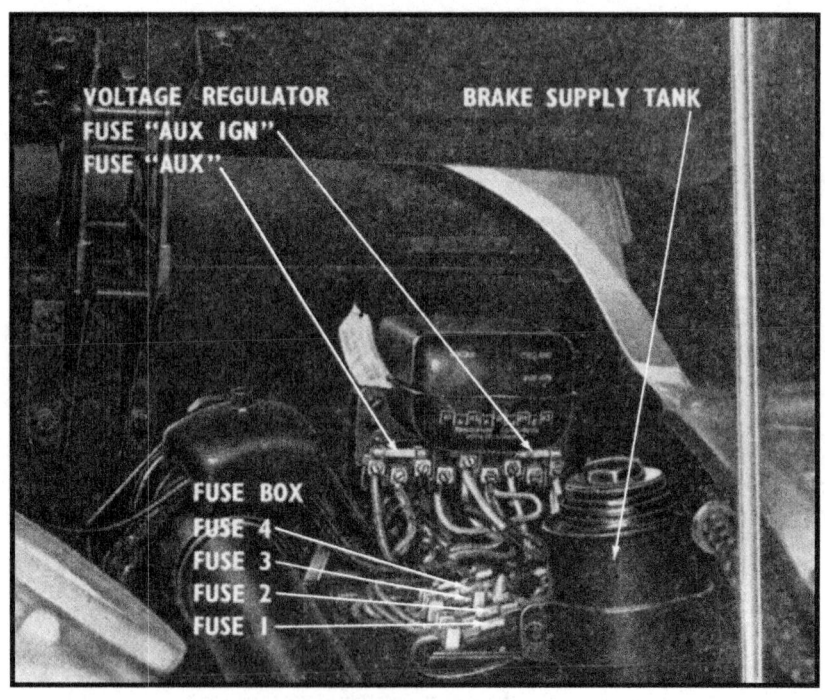

Plate 21. Fuses.

ENGINE

Air Cleaners. Every 5,000 miles (8,000 kilometres) or more frequently in dusty conditions, remove the air cleaner/s and thoroughly rinse in petrol. Before refitting, wet gauze with engine oil.

On the Fixed Head Coupe the air cleaner is situated forward of the radiator.

Carburetter and Fuel Pump Filters. Every 5,000 miles (8,000 kilometres) remove and clean the filters situated at the float chamber unions. Every 10,000 miles (16,000 kilometres) clean the filter situated in the base of the petrol pump. The petrol pump is situated on the rear of the chassis central cross member at the right-hand side. Remove six cheese-headed screws and withdraw base plate to gain access to filter. Since the petrol pump is below petrol tank level the following procedure is recommended to prevent draining the petrol tank.

Attach a suitable length of rubber tubing to the door pillar at a height above the petrol tank and pass the tube over the end of the nipple, as soon as it is detached, to avoid loss of petrol.

Carburetter Dash Pot Chambers. Every 2,500 miles (4,000 kilometres) remove caps on top of dash pots and fill piston spindle chambers with recommended grade of engine oil. Absence of oil will cause weakness of mixture on acceleration and poor performance. (Plate 32.)

PART II. MAINTENANCE INSTRUCTIONS

Distributor. Every 2,500 miles (4,000 kilometres) remove cover and rotor arm. Add one or two drops of engine oil in the centre hole on top of the shaft, and one drop to the contact breaker arm pivot. Give two or three drops to the centrifugal advance mechanism. Put a light smear of grease on the cam. Check contact breaker point gaps and adjust, if necessary, to ·012" (·31 mm.). Clean and refit distributor cover, check tightness of all connections (Plate 22).

Fan Bearings. Every 2,500 miles (4,000 kilometres) sparingly lubricate bearings through nipple provided using recommended lubricant (Plate 23).

Fan Belt. Every 5,000 miles (8,000 kilometres) check the tension of the fan belt and adjust if necessary. Adjustment is effected by loosening

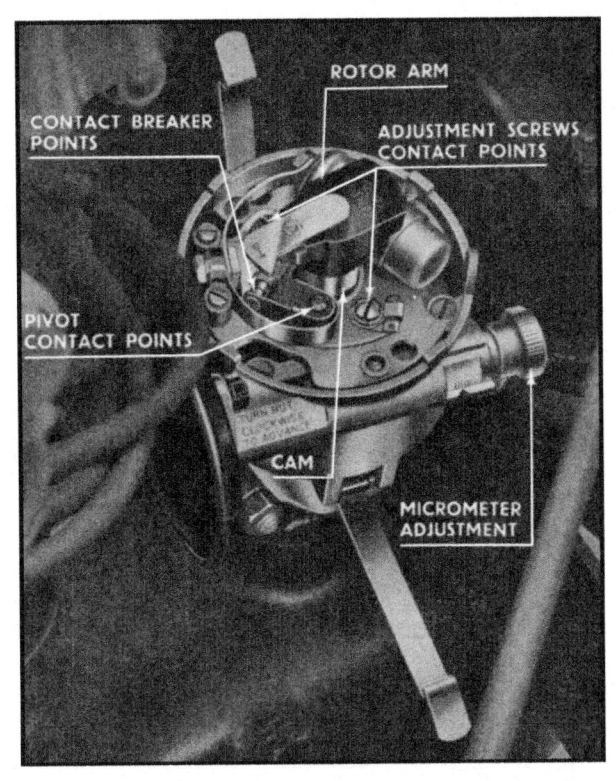

Plate 22. Distributor.

the dynamo adjusting bolt and both mounting bolts and levering the dynamo until belt tension is just obtained Tighten bolts. Undue tension will create heavy wear of belt, pulleys and dynamo bearings (Plate 23).

Oil Filter. Every 2,500 miles (4,000 kilometres) when the engine oil is changed, thoroughly rinse the oil filter element in petrol. Renew the element every 5,000 miles (8,000 kilometres) (Plate 24).

Oil Sump. Every 2,500 miles (4,000 kilometres) drain and refill the sump. New

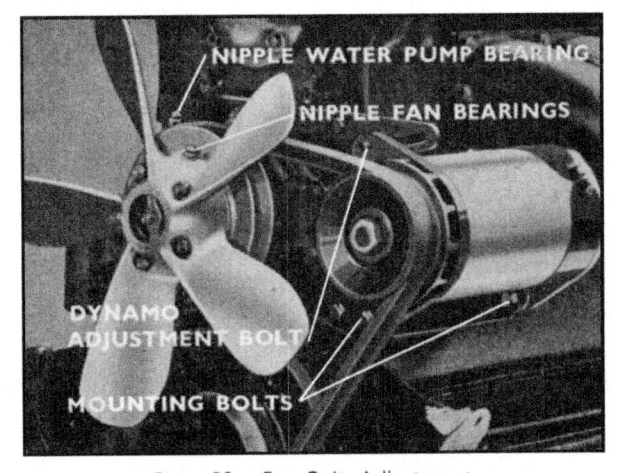

Plate 23. Fan Belt Adjustment.

engines should have the oil changed initially at 500 miles (800 kilometres). See Service Voucher. It is advantageous to carry out draining at the end of a run when the oil is hot and consequently more fluid.

Sparking Plugs. Every 5,000 miles (8,000 kilometres) remove, clean and test

PART II. MAINTENANCE INSTRUCTIONS

plugs, using Champion plug cleaning and testing equipment. Adjust gaps to ·022" (·56 mm.).

Water Pump. Every 2,500 miles (4,000 kilometres) lubricate the water pump bearing sparingly through the nipple provided using recommended lubricant (Plate 23).

FRONT SUSPENSION

The front suspension wishbones and radius arms are supported on rubber bonded bushes which require no lubrication. No attention is required to the torsion bar springs or anti-roll bar.

GEARBOX

Every 2,500 miles (4,000 kilometres) check the level of oil in the gearbox by means of the dipstick when the car is standing on level ground. Access is gained to the dipstick through the inspection plate situated in front of the gear lever (Plates 4 and 5). If necessary, top up through the dipstick hole with the recommended grade of oil.

Plate 24. Oil Filter.

Every 10,000 miles (16,000 kilometres) drain, flush out with flushing oil, and refill the gearbox with the recommended grade of oil. The square headed drain plug is situated at the base of the gearbox. It is advanatageous to carry out draining at the end of a run when the oil is hot and consequently more fluid.

OIL CAN LUBRICATION

Every 5,000 miles (8,000 kilometres) carry out oil can lubrication of the following:—

    Clutch pedal shaft.

    Front seat runners and adjustment mechanism.

    Hand brake ratchet mechanism.

    Door hinges and lock mechanisms.

    Boot lid hinges and lock.

    Windscreen wiper arm pivots.

    Bonnet hinges and catches.

    Accelerator pedal and throttle linkage.

    Petrol filler cover lock and hinges.

    Rear wing valance catches.

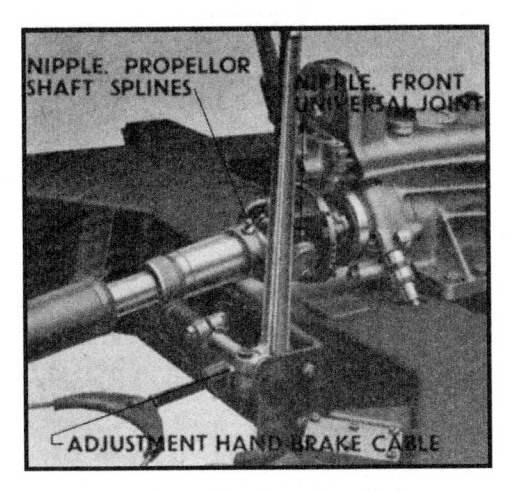

PART II. MAINTENANCE INSTRUCTIONS

PROPELLER SHAFT

Every 2,500 miles (4,000 kilometres) lubricate the nipples on the propeller shaft with recommended lubricant. The number of nipples and their location is as follows:—

| 1 Nipple. | Splines. |
| 2 Nipples. | Universal Joints. |

REAR AXLE

Every 2,500 miles (4,000 kilometres) check the level of the oil in the rear axle differential when the car is standing on level ground.

Plate 25. Propeller Shaft.

A combined level and filler plug is fitted to the cover plate or, alternatively, a dipstick and filler on the top of the nose of the differential. Top up, if necessary, to the bottom of this plug (see Plate 26) with the recommended grade of lubricant.

Since hypoid oils of different brands may not mix satisfactorily, draining and refilling is preferable to topping up if the brand of oil in the axle is unknown. New rear axles should have the oil changed initially at 500 miles (800 kilometres) (see Service Voucher) and subsequently every 10,000 miles (16,000 kilometres) drain flush out with flushing oil, and refill with the recommended grade of lubricant. The drain plug is situated at the base of the differential. The oil will drain more readily if the operation is carried out at the end of a journey when the oil is hot and consequently more fluid.

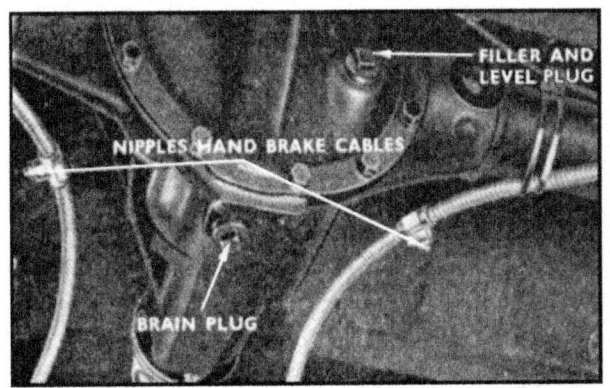

Plate 26. Rear Axle.

REAR SUSPENSION

Every 10,000 miles (16,000 kilometres) thoroughly clean the rear shock absorbers, examine the fluid level and top up, if necessary, using the recommended grade of fluid. The filler is situated on top of the shock absorber body and the body should be completely filled. Since grit or dirt will damage the shock absorber movement it is vitally important to clean thoroughly before removing the filler plug.

The rear springs are fitted with rubber bonded bushes at anchor bolts and shackles which should not be lubricated.

Every 2,500 miles (4,000 kilometres) lubricate the rear springs, through the four nipples provided on the gaiters, using the recommended lubricant.

PART II. MAINTENANCE INSTRUCTIONS

STEERING

Every 2,500 miles (4,000 kilometres) top up the steering box (Plate 27) and idle lever housing, if necessary, through the filler plug provided. Care should be taken to identify the steering box filler plug correctly. Top up the idle lever bearing housing, if necessary, with the recommended lubricant through the $\frac{5}{8}''$ hexagon plug situated on top (Plate 29).

Every 2,500 miles (4,000 kilometres) lubricate the four nipples on the joints of the steering linkage and the two nipples on the wheel swivels with the recommended lubricant. (Plate 29).

Plate 27. Steering Box Filler Plug.

The number of nipples and their location is as follows:—

2 Nipples. Tie rod (right hand).   1 Nipple. Wheel swivel (right hand).
2 Nipples. Tie rod (left hand).   1 Nipple. Wheel swivel (left hand).

TYRES

Every week check the tyre pressures with an approved tyre pressure gauge and adjust the pressures to front 25 lbs. per sq. in., rear 25 lbs. per sq. in. (1·8 kg./cm.²). Ensure that all valves are fitted with valve caps.

Periodically remove all flints and chips from the tyres and check that all wheel nuts are tight.

For fast driving conditions where comfort is not of primary importance maintain pressures at 35 lbs. per sq. in. front, and 35 lbs. per sq. in. rear (2·5 kg./cm.²).

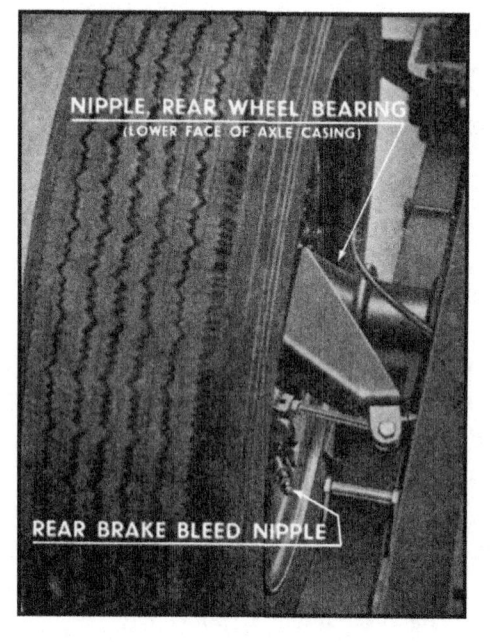

WHEEL BEARINGS

Front. Every 5,000 miles (8,000 kilometres) lubricate the front wheel bearings sparingly with recommended lubricant through the nipples provided. The Nipples are situated on the wheel hub and are accessible when the front wheels are removed (Plate 19). A bleed hole is provided in the cap to indicate when an excess of lubricant has been applied.

Rear. Every 5,000 miles (8,000 kilometres) lubricate the rear wheel bearings sparingly with recommended lubricant through the nipples provided. The nipples are situated on the bottom face of the axle casing immediately behind the brake back plate (Plate 28).

A bleed hole is provided on the top face of the axle casing to indicate when an excess of lubricant has been applied.

Plate 28. Nipple—Rear Wheel Bearing.

PART II. MAINTENANCE INSTRUCTIONS

Plate 29. Nipples—Steering.

PART III. SERVICE INSTRUCTIONS

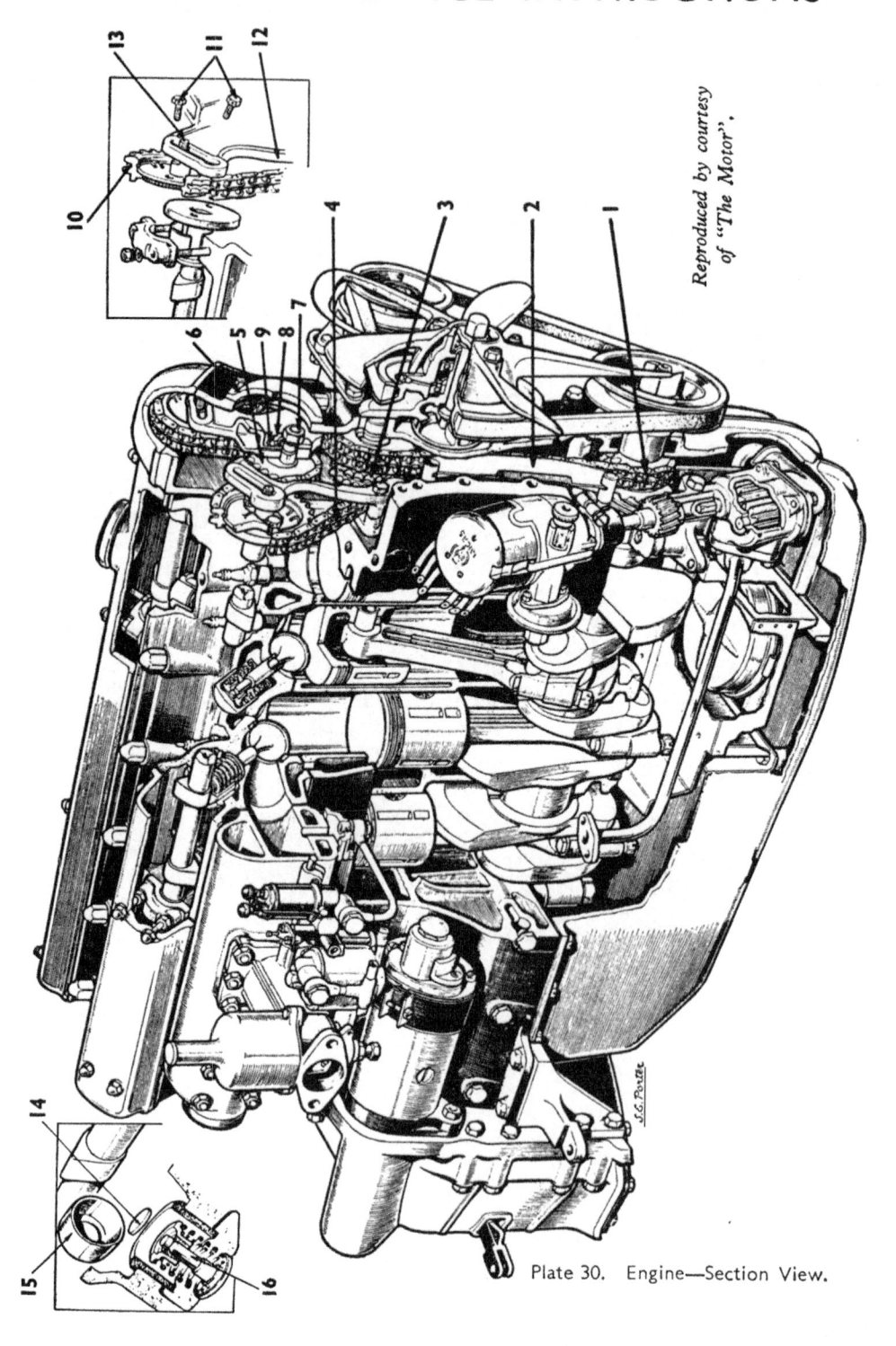

Plate 30. Engine—Section View.

PART III. SERVICE INSTRUCTIONS

ENGINE

Decarbonising and Grinding Valves. Before decarbonising is undertaken it is desirable to obtain a set comprising all the gaskets and joints which will be required when assembling. A kit containing this material is available from any Jaguar Distributor or Dealer by ordering Assembly No. 311.

TUNE-UP DATA

Valve clearances (set when cold)	Inlet ·006" (·15 mm.).
	Exhaust ·008" (·20 mm.).
Sparking plug gap	·022" (·56 mm.).
Distributor contact point gap ..	·012" (·31 mm.).
Ignition timing (7 : 1 and 8 : 1 compression ratios)	Set to fire 5° B.T.D.C. with both the vacuum and centrifugal advance mechanisms in the fully retard position.

General. The drive for the twin overhead camshafts is primarily by duplex chain (1) with automatic tension device (2) from crankshaft to a shaft fitted at the top of the front face of the cylinder block. A second sprocket (3) on this shaft drives the camshafts by duplex chain (4), an eccentric idler (5) being provided for adjustment purposes.

Access to the idler adjustment is gained by removing the breather housing (6) Adjustment is effected by a locknut (7) and serrated adjuster plate (8) with spring-loaded stop peg (9).

The camshaft chain wheels (10) are attached to the camshafts by setscrews (11) and when removed may be attached to support brackets (12) by a nut fitted to guide pins (13), thus allowing free removal of the cylinder head and camshafts without disturbing the valve timing.

Valve adjustment is effected by adjusting pads (14) fitted between valve inserts (15) and valves (16). (See Plate 30.)

Disconnect Engine Connections. Disconnect battery lead. Drain cooling system by opening radiator drain tap and conserve water if anti-freeze is in use.

Remove air cleaners.

Disconnect throttle linkage at flexible coupling at bulkhead and remove throttle linkage return spring.

Disconnect distributor vacuum feed pipe from front carburetter.

Disconnect both leads from self-starting carburetter solenoid and solenoid feed lead from clip at rear of induction manifold.

Disconnect petrol feed pipe at float chamber unions.

Disconnect revolution counter cable from rear of left-hand camshaft.

Disconnect top water hose from water manifold.

Remove high tension leads from sparking plugs and lead carrier from cylinder head studs. Remove sparking plugs.

Disconnect engine breather pipe from breather housing.

Disconnect both exhaust down pipes from manifolds.

Disconnect both camshaft oil feed pipes from rear of cylinder head.

PART III. SERVICE INSTRUCTIONS

Remove Cylinder Head. Remove eight dome nuts from each camshaft cover and lift off covers.

Remove four nuts securing breather housing and withdraw housing observing position of baffle plate with oil drain aperture at the bottom. Release tension on camshaft chain by slackening nut on eccentric idler sprocket shaft, depressing spring-loaded stop peg and rotating serrated adjuster plate clockwise. Anti-clockwise rotation of the serrated adjuster viewed from the front of the engine tightens the chain.

Break locking wire on two setscrews securing chain wheels to respective camshafts. Mark relationship of chain wheel and camshaft to facilitate assembly, remove setscrews and withdraw chain wheel with chain in position. (Do not disturb the circlip retaining chain wheel to the adjuster plate to avoid necessity of valve timing on assembly.)

The two camshaft chain wheels may now be slid up the support brackets, and retained in this position by a nut fitted to the guide pin. Remove fourteen cylinder head dome nuts and six nuts securing the front of the cylinder head to cylinder block.

Lift off cylinder head complete with exhaust manifolds, inlet manifolds and carburetters. Remove and scrap cylinder head gasket.

Remove Valves. With the cylinder head on the bench remove inlet manifold complete with carburetters and both exhaust manifolds.

Remove four bearing caps from each camshaft and lift out camshafts (note mating marks on bearing caps).

Remove twelve floating tappets and adjusting pads situated between tappets and valve stems.

Obtain a block of wood the approximate size of the combustion chambers and place this under the valve heads in No. 1 cylinder. Press down the valve collars and extract the split cotters. Remove collars, valves, springs and spring seats. Repeat for the remaining five cylinders. Valves are numbered and must be replaced in original locations, No. 1 cylinder being at the rear, that is, the flywheel end.

Decarbonise and Grind Valves. Remove all traces of carbon from the combustion chambers and deposits from carburetter ports, exhaust ports and induction passages. The cylinder head is of aluminium alloy and great care should be exercised not to damage this with scrapers or sharp pointed tools. Use worn emery cloth and paraffin only. Thoroughly clean the water passages in the cylinder head. Clean the carbon deposits from the piston crowns and ensure that the top face of the cylinder block is quite clean particularly round the cylinder head studs. Remove any pitting in valve seats using valve seat grinding equipment. Reface the valves, if necessary, using valve grinding equipment ; grind the valves to the seats using a suction valve grinding tool. Valve seat angle : exhaust 45°, inlet 30°.

Clean the sparking plugs by sandblasting and set gaps to ·022" (·56 mm.). (If possible use approved plug cleaning and testing equipment.) Clean and adjust distributor contact breaker points to ·012" (·31 mm.).

Adjusting Valve Clearances. Thoroughly clean all traces of valve grinding compound from cylinder head and valve gear. Assemble valves in head and replace camshafts. Obtain and record all valve clearances by using a feeler gauge between

PART III.   SERVICE INSTRUCTIONS

the back of each cam and the appropriate valve tappet. Correct clearances are: inlet ·006" (·15 mm.), exhaust ·008" (·20 mm.).

Adjusting pads are available rising in ·001" (·03 mm.) sizes from ·085" to ·103" (2·16 to 2·61 mm.) and are acid etched on the surface with the letters A to S, each letter indicating an increase in size of ·001" (·03 mm).

Should any valve clearance require correction remove the appropriate camshaft, valve tappet and adjusting pad. Observe the letter etched on the existing adjusting pad and should the recorded clearance for this valve, obtained previously, have shown, say, ·002" (·05 mm.) excessive clearance, select a new adjusting pad bearing a letter two higher than that removed. If the recorded clearance was, say, ·002" (·05 mm.) less than recommended clearance, then the new adjusting pad should bear a letter two lower than the original pad.

As an example, assume that No. 1 inlet valve clearance is tested and recorded as ·009" (·23 mm.). On removal of adjusting pad, if this is etched with the letter D, then substitution with a pad bearing the letter G will correct the clearance for No. 1 inlet valve.

Reassembly. When all valve clearances have been correctly set refit exhaust manifolds and induction manifold complete with carburetters.

Before refitting the cylinder head it is important to observe that if the camshafts are out of phase with piston position fouling may take place between inlet valves and pistons. It is, therefore, essential to adhere to the following procedure before fitting the cylinder head :—

(a) Turn the camshafts, one at a time, until the keyways cut in the front flange of the shafts are vertical to the camshaft housing face and accurately position by engaging valve timing gauge provided in tool kit. Key of gauge locates in keyway of camshaft and bottom face of gauge with face of camshaft housing on cylinder head.

(b) Turn No. 6 (front) piston to firing position on top dead centre. A timing hole is provided in the clutch bell housing at a point immediately below the left hand camshaft. Line up the arrow on the flywheel with the datum line cut on the cylinder block which will position No. 6 piston at top dead centre. Remove distributor cover and check that rotor arm is opposite No. 6 cylinder segment.

Refit the cylinder head using a new cylinder head gasket fitted side marked "TOP" upwards and lightly smeared with jointing compound. When tightening cylinder head nuts it is recommended that a torque spanner should be used and the nuts tightened at a torque setting of 650 lbs. ins.

Reassembly is the reverse of the above instructions ensuring that the camshaft chain wheels are bolted to the camshafts with the marks previously mentioned in line (it will be appreciated that the chain wheels can be bolted up 180° out of phase with the camshafts). Finally locate the chain wheel setscrews with new locking wires.

Before refitting the breather housing adjust the camshaft chain with the eccentric sprocket by rotating the serrated adjuster as far as it will go in an anti-clockwise direction. Rock engine in both directions and check by hand the tightness of the chain on both outer sides below the camshaft chain wheels. Some flexibility of the chain should be felt, that is, the chain must not be dead tight. If necessary set back the adjuster one or more serrations to relieve any excess tightness. Securely tighten the locknut (see Plate 31).

PART III. SERVICE INSTRUCTIONS

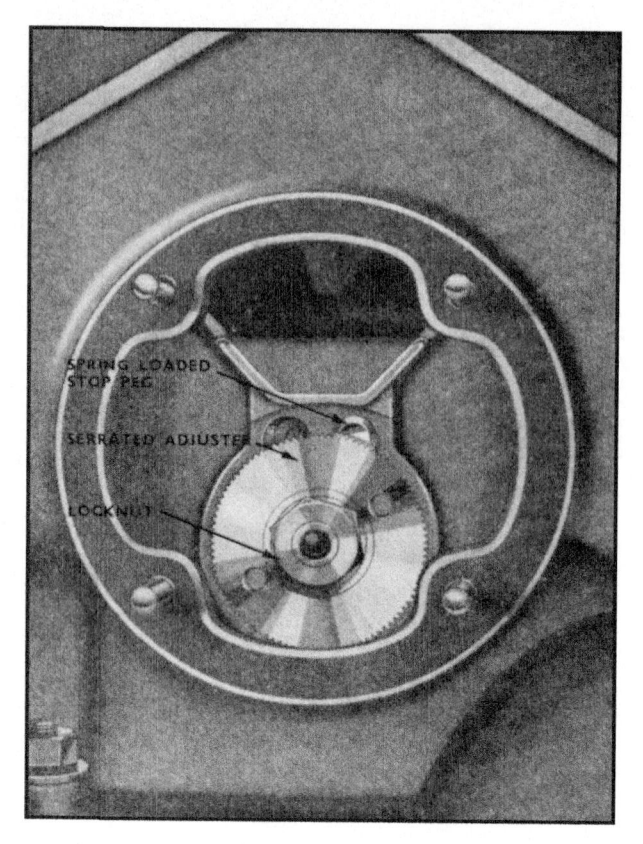

Plate 31. Timing Chain Adjustment.

ENGINE TIGHTENING TORQUE DATA

Flywheel	800 lbs. ins.
Connecting Rod	450 lbs. ins.
Cylinder Head	650 lbs. ins.
Main Bearings	1,000 lbs. ins.
Camshaft Bearings	175 lbs. ins.

CARBURETTER TUNING

GENERAL

It is useless to attempt carburetter tuning until the cylinder compressions, valve clearances, sparking plug gaps and contact breaker point gaps have been tested, checked and adjusted if necessary. The distributor centrifugal advance mechanism and vacuum advance operation should be checked and ignition timing reset on the road so that the engine just shows a tendency to pink on full throttle under load at 1,500 to 2,000 r.p.m. in top gear. The ignition setting is important since if retarded or advanced too far the setting of the carburetters will be affected.

PART III. SERVICE INSTRUCTIONS

Plate 32. Carburetters.

TUNING (see Plate 32).

Only two adjustments are provided at the carburetters. (1) The throttle adjusting screws governing idling speed and (2) the jet adjusting screws governing mixture strength. Correct setting of the mixture strength at idling speed ensures that the carburetters are correctly adjusted throughout their entire range.

Ensure that both needles are correctly located in the pistons, that is, with the shoulder of the needles flush with the base of the pistons. Check over the carburetters and ensure that pistons are free in the dash pots, petrol filters clean and hydraulic piston dampers topped up with the recommended grade of engine oil. Lubricate throttle controls and check free operation and full travel.

Run the engine until normal operating temperature is reached and check that both carburetters are sucking equally by listening with the ear or placing the fingers partially over the intake so that the suction can be heard. Slacken one clamp bolt on the universally jointed connection between the throttle spindles. Rotate the throttle adjusting screws until the carburetters are synchronised, that is, are sucking equally, and the engine is idling at approximately 500 r.p.m. Tighten the clamp bolt. Before carrying out the instructions which follow, it is desirable to ensure that the mixture strength of both carburetters is approximately correct.

It may, therefore, be desirable to screw the jet adjusting screws upwards (clockwise) as far as they will go and then rotate them downwards (anti-clockwise) two and one-half turns, ensuring that the jets are not sticking and are following the movement of the adjusting screws.

PART III.   SERVICE INSTRUCTIONS

Next check the mixture strength by starting the engine and operate the piston lifting pin of the *front* carburetter and so lift the piston approximately $\frac{1}{4}$" (6·0 mm.) when, if:—

(a)   The engine speed increases and the engine continues to run at increased speed this indicates that the mixture strength of the *rear* carburetter is too rich.

(b)   The engine speed increases and the engine then stops this indicates that the mixture strength of the *rear* carburetter is too weak.

(c)   The engine speed increases momentarily and then decreases but the engine continues to run somewhat bumpily, then the strength mixture of the *rear* carburetter is correct.

Repeat the operation lifting the rear carburetter piston and testing the mixture setting of the front carburetter.

To adjust the mixture strength remove the dome nut covering the jet and to enrich the mixture rotate the jet adjusting screw in an anti-clockwise direction, that is, downwards. To weaken the mixture rotate the jet adjusting screw clockwise, that is, upwards. Ensure that the jet is not sticking and is following the movement of the adjusting screw. Always replace the dome nuts after adjustment.

Some slight adjustment of the slow running, to maintain this at 500 r.p.m. may now be necessary following alteration of the mixture strength in which case ensure that the two throttle adjusting screws are rotated by an exactly equal amount or the adjustments previously made will be upset.

ENGINE, CLUTCH AND GEARBOX REMOVAL

In the event of it being necessary to carry out a repair to one of the above units note that the gearbox may be removed from the engine when the floorboards have been removed and the rear of the engine supported.

Removal of the gearbox will give access to the clutch.

The engine and gearbox may be removed together as a unit when the radiator has been removed, the ancillary equipment disconnected and the gear lever removed.

FRONT SHOCK ABSORBERS

The Newton front shock absorbers are pre-filled and require no topping up with fluid in normal service.

In the event of the unit being dismantled, however, note that when reassembling, the unit must be filled with 130 c.c. of one of the following fluids:—

Vacuum	Wakefield	Shell	Essolube	Price's
Mobil Shock	Castrol	Shell	Esso Shock	Energol
Absorber Oil	Shockol	Donax	Absorber Oil	S.A.
Light		A.1		Light

BRAKES

To Bleed System. As a tandem type master cylinder is fitted, the best result will be obtained if one front and one rear wheel cylinder are bled simultaneously.

Slacken rear brake shoe adjusters to zero position. Place the hand brake in the 'OFF' position. Fill up the supply tank with fluid, exercising great care to prevent entry of dirt.

Take one front and one rear brake at a time, fit rubber bleed tubes to bleeder nipples and allow them to hang in clean containers or glass jars. Unscrew the nipples about three-quarters of a turn and operate the brake pedal its full travel a few times, allowing two or three seconds between each stroke. Pumping must be continued until the fluid is entirely free of air, care being taken to see that the reservoir is replenished frequently during this operation, for should it be allowed to empty, more air will enter. After expelling all traces of air, hold brake pedal

PART III. SERVICE INSTRUCTIONS

in depressed position and tighten nipples. Repeat procedure on the other two brakes.

SPARKING PLUGS

The normal life of a sparking plug is approximately 10,000 miles and when replacements are necessary these should be of the same type as originally fitted, namely Champion Type N.A.8. for 8 to 1 compression ratio engines, and Champion L.10 S for 7 to 1 compression ratio engines.

The correct gap setting for these plugs is ·022" (·56 mm.) which gap should be set using a feeler gauge and by bending the side or earth electrode. In no circumstances attempt to bend the centre electrode, which action may split the insulator.

When refitting sparking plugs, ensure that the copper washers are not defective. If worn and flattened fit new ones. Paint splashes, accumulation of oil and dust, etc., on the top half of the insulator can be the cause of unsatisfactory performance. Plug insulators should be wiped with a clean rag at regular intervals. Clean the spark plugs by air blasting with plug cleaning equipment at the intervals recommended in the Maintenance List.

FRONT SUSPENSION—ADJUSMENT OF TORSION RODS

General. Two torsion rods are fitted, running longitudinally, one on either side of the chassis frame members. Both ends of these rods are splined, the front coupling to the rear lower wishbone member with a splined muff held by two set bolts, whilst the rear carries a lever transmitting reaction to the centre chassis cross member through a bolt which at the same time serves for adjustment of load.

To check for correct setting, proceed as follows:—

Place the car on a dead level surface with wheels in straight-ahead position and tyre pressures at 25 lbs. per sq. in. (1·8 kg./cm.²) front, and 25 lbs. per sq. in. (1·8 kg./cm.²) rear. Load car with two 100 lb. weights (90·7 kilos.) placed in a position as near as possible to that occupied by driver and passenger. These conditions being fulfilled, a 7⅛" (180·9 mm.) test piece should just pass under the lower face of the chassis side member immediately behind the engine sump.

Adjustment. Should adjustment be necessary, first of all verify the position of the rear reaction lever locking set bolt with relation to the slot cut in the cross member, and note that clockwise rotation of the brass adjusting nut will increase torsion in the rod, moving the lock bolt to the top of the slot and raise the car. Anti-clockwise motion will have the reverse effect. Adjustment should only be carried out with the locking bolt released and the front of the car jacked up to reduce load on the adjustment nuts to a minimum.

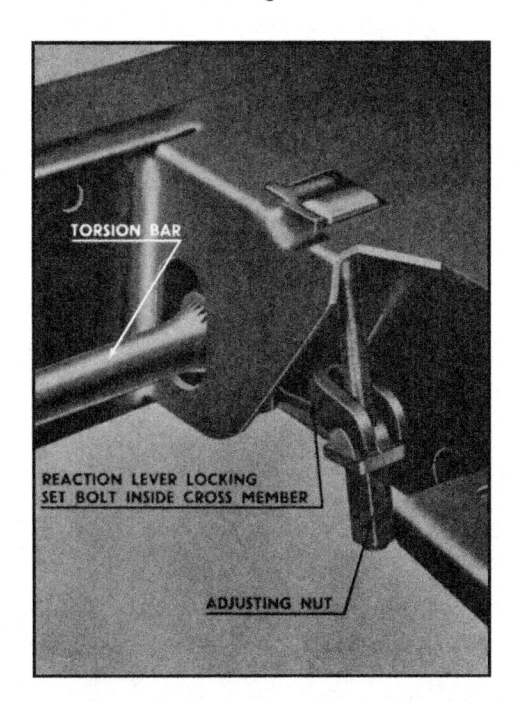

Plate 33. Torsion Rod Adjustment.

PART III.   SERVICE INSTRUCTIONS

Should it not be possible to obtain a correct setting within the limits of the slot, then it will be necessary to reposition the torsion rod in relation to the lower rear wishbone member, noting that, when viewed from the front, turning the offside (right hand) splined muff in an anti-clockwise rotation will increase torsion, that is, raise the car, and turning it clockwise will decrease torsion, that is, lower the car. Conversely, turning the nearside (left hand) muff clockwise will increase, or anti-clockwise decrease torsion.

It is important to note that, should correction be required on both torsion rods, then adjustment should take place a little at a time on each until the required results are obtained, finally retightening the locking set bolts.

Camber. Insert four $7\frac{1}{8}''$ (18·1 cm.) test pieces between the chassis frame and the ground at the forward and rear ends of the parallel section of the frame.

Jack up the rear of the car, remove rear road wheels and lower until the chassis frame rests on the two rear test pieces. Load the front of the car until the chassis frame rests on the two front test pieces.

Line up the front wheel being checked parallel to the centre line of the car. Using an approved camber gauge, check camber. Rotate the wheel being checked through 180°, and recheck. Camber should be $1\frac{3}{4}°$-2° positive.

Adjusting is effected by removing or adding shims between the chassis frame side members and the front suspension top wishbone brackets. Inserting shims increases; removing shims decreases camber. It should be noted that $\frac{1}{16}''$ (1·6 mm.) of shimming equals approximately $\frac{1}{2}°$ of camber. (See Plate 34.)

Check the other front wheel in a similar manner.

Castor. Insert four $7\frac{1}{8}''$ (18·1 cm.) test pieces between the chassis frame and the ground at the forward and rear ends of the parallel section of the frame.

Jack up the rear of the car, remove rear road wheels and lower until the chassis frame rests on the two rear test pieces. Load the front of the car until the chassis frame rests on the two front test pieces.

Using an approved castor gauge check castor, which should be as follows:—

Castor   ..   ..   3° Postive.

To alter castor, slack back two bolts securing the front suspension upper wishbone members to the stub axle carrier and either remove or add shims from front to rear or rear to front as necessary. To increase negative castor, remove shims from front of member and insert in rear, and to increase positive castor, remove shims from rear and insert in front. It should be noted that $\frac{1}{16}''$ (1·6 mm.) of shimming will alter castor by approximately $\frac{1}{4}°$ in either direction. Tighten the two bolts loosened for purposes of extracting shims. (See Plate 34.)

The front of the car should be jacked up when turning the wheels from lock to lock during checking.

PART III. SERVICE INSTRUCTIONS

Plate No. 34. Castor and Camber Adjustments.

FRONT AND REAR HUB RACES—ADJUSTMENT AND SERVICING
Front Hubs.

General. The races fitted to front hubs are of the Timken tapered roller type, adjustable for initial assembly, and also to re-establish correct clearance when this has increased due to normal wear.

Adjustment. Jack up wheel, remove nave plate and wheel. Prise grease retaining cap from hub centre, thus exposing pin and slotted nut by which adjustment is effected. Withdraw split pin and tighten nut to decrease or slacken to increase clearance. Desired end float is ·005″ (·13 mm.). Ensure that split pin is inserted correctly when adjustment has been made and replace grease retaining cap.

PART III. SERVICE INSTRUCTIONS

Lubrication. Pack hub with grease by applying gun to nipples provided until excess exudes from bleed hole drilled in the cap. Replace road wheel, nuts and nave plate and remove jack from axle.

Rear Hubs.

General. Rear hub bearings are of the single Timken tapered roller type, the inner members of which are located on the axle shafts. As both axle shafts butt against a sliding spacer block, adjustment of one race will affect the clearance of the other. Adjustment is by means of shims located between race housing and brake back plate. The combined end float (bearing clearance) is ·006"—·008" (·15 mm.—·20 mm.) and it is essential to ensure that an equal number of shims are fitted to either side in order to maintain centralisation of half shafts.

Adjustment. Jack up rear axle, remove nave plates and wheels. Remove two countersunk screws retaining brake drum to axle shaft flange and ease drum off register. Remove cotter pins and five nuts securing rear hub housing to axle casing and ease axle shaft away from casing, thus exposing the adjusting shims between hub bearing housing and brake back plate. Remove or add shims until the limits of ·006"—·008" (·15 mm.—·20 mm.) are obtained. When the correct clearance has been obtained, replace five nuts and bolts, tighten, and replace cotter pins. Check clearance again after final tightening. Replace brake drums, countersunk setscrews, wheels and nave plates. Lower car off jack.

Lubrication. Pack hub bearings with recommended lubricant by applying gun to nipples situated at extremities of the axle casing. To prevent over-filling, bleed holes are provided in the axle casing.

ADJUSTMENT OF STEERING TRACK AND STEERING LOCK

Steering Track.

General. The track rod is of the divided type, comprising two short, equal length outer members carried on normal ball joints and coupled to a centre member by means of couplings provided with rubber bonded bearings. One bearing is located in the steering arm, whilst the other is located in the steering idle lever, which runs in a long thread bearing.

Adjustment. Place the car on a dead level surface with wheels in straight-ahead position. Check tyres for correct inflation, pressures being front 25 lbs. per sq. in. (1·8 kg./cm.^{2}), and rear 25 lbs. per sq. in. (1·8 kg./cm.^{2}). Assemble track setting gauge and check setting; this should be $\frac{1}{8}$" minimum to $\frac{3}{16}$" minimum (3·18 mm. to 4·76 mm.) toe in. If adjustment is required, slacken off clamp bolts at either end of central member and rotate as required. Retighten clamp bolts.

Steering Lock. Steering lock control is provided by setscrews mounted in brackets situated on the front chassis cross member.

Rotate the setscrews to a position which allows $\frac{1}{4}$" (6·35 mm.) clearance between the wheel and chassis on full lock. Secure the setscrews in this position with the locknuts provided.

STEERING UNIT

General. The steering unit is of the high efficiency, recirculating ball type, in which motion is transmitted from column to rocker shaft through a sliding member running on a continuous train of ball bearings. The single start worm on the lower end of the inner column is supported at either end by crowded ball races, correctly adjusted by means of shims placed between end cover and casing. The upper end

PART III.   SERVICE INSTRUCTIONS

of the inner column is located in a fabric oilless bush and oil impregnated felt washer, needing neither adjustment nor lubrication. Formed on the sliding member is a conical abutment, mating with similar faces on the rocker shaft, and a bearing pin carrying a roller which runs in a slot in the cover plate.

Normally the only running adjustment required will be that of resetting the end float of the rocker shaft. Both the adjuster and the oil filler plug are fitted in the cover plate, the adjuster being identified by its screwed extension and locknut. (See Plate 27.)

Adjustment. Remove setscrew from adjuster and withdraw preloading spring. Screw down adjuster until it just touches the rocker shaft when this is in the straight-ahead position. It is most important that this position is maintained, for the conical faces are so designed to give slightly more backlash towards full lock. Having arrived at the correct adjustment with no end float on the rocker shaft, lock up the adjuster and replace the preloading spring and setscrew.

Jack up the front wheels, preferably under each suspension unit, and check the steering for freedom of rotation, from one full lock to the other.

SUSPENSION RUBBER BUSHES—SERVICING

General. Various types of rubber bushes are used in the suspension and the application for the various assemblies is as follows:—

1. **Rear Springs.** Standard silentbloc bushes are fitted to the rear springs and shackles.

2. **Rear Shock Absorbers.** Link bushes of the normal type are pressed into the eye composite with assembly bolts.

3. **Front Suspension.** The wishbone assemblies are fitted with thin tapered rubber bushes to both top and bottom wishbone arms. The lower arm consists of two members, the main member is an 'I' section stamping extending at right angles to the frame and receives the wheel swivel bottom ball joint at its outer extremity. This main member is mounted on two opposed Metalastik conical bonded rubber bushes carried by a bracket attached to the underside of the chassis frame. The bracket is extended forward to receive a similar pair of bushes fitted to the boss of a stay rod running diagonally back to the outer end of the main arm.

   The upper arms are similarly mounted on opposed Metalastik conical bonded rubber bushes carried by a bracket attached to the top of the chassis frame side member.

4. **Front Shock Absorbers.** The top mountings comprise flat rubber washers trapped between steel washers and the mounting bracket. Harris type bushes are fitted on the lower link pin, preloaded by washer and inserted split pin.

Servicing. Whenever any of the above assemblies are dismantled either for examination or replacement it is essential that the car is in the normal riding position, either before preloading is applied to any of the rubber bushes mentioned above or assemblies finally locked up. If these precautions are not taken, excessive load will be applied with consequent damage and possible premature failure of rubber bushes. The rubber bushes should not in any circumstances be lubricated.

PART III.   SERVICE INSTRUCTIONS

WINDSCREEN

To Remove and Refit. The windscreen assembly is mounted so that it can be removed quickly and easily should it be desired to operate the car without the screen.

Remove windscreen wiper arms and blades by releasing the nut securing them to the operating spindles. Remove dash casing. The screen pillars are retained by two bolts at either end and a nut under the centre pillar, all situated behind the dash. Withdraw the bolts and nut and lift the screen assembly upwards.

Alternatively, the driver's or passenger's individual screen may be withdrawn by removing three screws retaining the hood centre catch and two screws passing through the side pillars and sliding the individual screen out of the main frame.

Refitting in both cases is the reverse of the above procedure.

SERVICE DEPARTMENTS

SERVICE

Address your enquiries to :

SERVICE DEPARTMENT
JAGUAR CARS LIMITED, COVENTRY

Telephone No. 88681

Your car has the Chassis Number stamped on a plate on the right side of the dash giving engine and chassis numbers. Both these numbers should be quoted when enquiries are made, and as a further check, horse power and year of manufacture should also be given.

Should your car require service see the dealer from whom the car was purchased. If you are on tour apply to the nearest Jaguar Dealer.

LONDON SERVICE DEPARTMENT

Owners in or near London are advised that a special Jaguar Service Department, is maintained by Messrs. Henlys Ltd., sole London Distributors for Jaguar Cars. This service department is fully equipped to deal with every kind of repair and overhaul, an expert staff of trained mechanics being retained solely for Jaguar service work. Enquiries should be addressed to :

MESSRS. HENLYS LTD.

Jaguar Service Department
Great West Road, Brentford, Middlesex
Telephone No. Ealing 3477

Should the owner obtain the handbook without having first obtained a guarantee form, he should apply to the dealer, who will supply the necessary form.

When this is obtained, fill in the bottom paragraph and send the whole document to the Guarantee Department as soon after purchase of the car as possible. Guarantee claims are not accepted by our Service Department unless the completed forms are in their possession.

SPARE PARTS

Direct issue of spare parts is not made from the factory.

Requirements should be obtained or ordered through the nearest Jaguar Distributor or Dealer.

ACCESSORIES AND EQUIPMENT

Proprietary equipment as fitted to Jaguar Cars can either be obtained direct from the manufacturers, whose addresses are given below, or will be supplied by the Spares Department, Jaguar Cars Ltd., at list prices current from time to time.

All claims for replacement or alleged defective parts must be referred direct to the respective manufacturers to be dealt with under the terms of their guarantee.

Component	Manufacturers
Lighting, Ignition and Starting Equipment Windscreen Wiper Electric Horns	Joseph Lucas Ltd., Great King St., Birmingham.
Rear Shock Absorbers	Girling Ltd., Kings Rd., Tyseley, Birmingham 11.
Front Shock Absorbers	Newton & Bennett Ltd., Valetta Rd., Acton, London, W.3.
Speedometer Revolution Counter Oil Pressure and Water Temperature Gauge Petrol Gauge, Cigar Lighter Clock	Smith's Motor Accessories Ltd., Cricklewood Works, London, N.W.2.
Carburetters Fuel Pump	Messrs. S. U. Carburetter Co. Ltd., Wood Lane, Erdington, Birmingham, 24.
Tyres	Dunlop Rubber Co. Ltd., Fort Dunlop, Erdington, Birmingham.
Road Wheels	Dunlop Rim & Wheel Co. Ltd., Holbrook Lane, Coventry.
Steering Unit	Burman & Sons Ltd., Wychall Lane, King's Norton, Birmingham, 20.
Brakes	Lockheed Hydraulic Brakes, Automotive Products Co. Ltd., Tachbrook Rd., Leamington Spa.

Proprietary articles, which are considered to be defective, returned to our works will be forwarded to the component manufacturer concerned. Should immediate replacement be required the parts will be charged for, but will be credited if the component manufacturer accepts responsibility under the guarantee or manufacturer's reasons for non-supply under guarantee will be submitted.

COPY OF GUARANTEE

On the sale or supply of all motor cars and goods by Jaguar Cars Ltd. (called "the Company") and on the carrying out of all repairs and work by them all guarantees, warranties or conditions (including any condition as to quality or fitness for any particular purpose) whether express, or implied by Statute, Common Law or otherwise, are excluded, and hereby expressly negatived.

In lieu of such express or implied conditions, warranties or guarantees the Company will give the following guarantee PROVIDED that the customer correctly fills up and signs the slip at the foot of this document and delivers this document with the attached slip so filled up and signed to the Company within seven days of the purchase by the customer of a Jaguar Car or goods. On receipt of this document so completed and signed the Company will return the top portion hereof to the customer.

It must be clearly understood that if a customer fails to comply with this preliminary condition the Company will be under no liability whatsoever either upon the following guarantee or upon any express or implied condition, warranty or guarantee.

MANUFACTURERS' GUARANTEE

In case of defect, breakage or breakdown of any motor car or goods supplied by the Company being discovered or occurring within SIX CALENDAR MONTHS from the date of sale, caused by defective workmanship or material (proved to the satisfaction of the Company) the defective part will be repaired or the Company will supply free of charge a new part in place thereof. Such period of six months is from the date of the supply by the Company of the motor car or goods, but if the motor car or goods are sold by a motor dealer and have not been previously used, the period starts from the date of supply by such dealer to the customer.

The Company's responsibility is limited to the conditions of this guarantee and the Company will not be liable for any damages or contingent or resulting liability or other loss arising through any breakdown, breakage or defect. The Company does not acknowledge any claim in respect of labour expenses including labour expended in dismantling or fitting arising from repairs, nor does it accept any responsibility for repairs or the fitting of replacement parts executed by Agents, or other repairers. The Company also will not be responsible for defect, breakage or breakdown caused by wear or tear, misuse or neglect. The judgment of the Company in all cases of claims shall be final and conclusive and the customer agrees to accept its decision on all questions as to defects and to the exchange of part or parts. After the expiration of six months from the despatch of notification of the Company's decision the part or parts submitted for inspection may be scrapped by the Company or returned to the customer carriage forward. The Company accepts no responsibility for any goods which have been altered after leaving the Company's works, or which have been used for motor racing or let out on hire or on or from which the Company's identification numbers or marks have been altered or removed. The Company accepts no responsibility for tyres, speedometers, electrical equipment, glass (or Safety Glass) or any other parts or accessories (other than for engines or chassis) which are not the Company's own manufacture. All claims of alleged defect in such items must be referred to the respective manufacturers direct. The Company accepts no responsibility on the sale of second-hand motor cars.

This guarantee is subject to the following conditions :—

CONDITIONS

1. This guarantee shall not be transferred to anyone unless the Company's consent in writing has been first obtained to such transfer.
2. The Company's guarantee shall not apply to any motor car or goods which have been purchased at any price other than the Company's current retail price at the time of sale.
3. Any motor car or goods alleged to be defective must be returned to the Guarantee Department of Jaguar Cars Ltd., at Foleshill, Coventry, carriage paid, and clearly labelled with the sender's name and address, within ten days of discovery of alleged defect. A letter under separate cover must at the same time be sent to the Guarantee Department giving the following details :—
   (a) Commission Number of the car.
   (b) The nature of the defect, breakage or breakdown which is alleged.
   (c) A brief description of all circumstances which will facilitate a quick and satisfactory settlement.
   (d) If there has been any correspondence or an invoice rendered the Company's reference number should be quoted.
4. Delivery of all goods supplied by the Company under this guarantee will be made at the Company's Works.
5. The term "Agent" where used is in a complimentary sense only and those persons or firms who are styled the Company's "Agents" are not authorised to advertise, incur any debts, transact any business, or incur any liabilities whatsoever on the Company's behalf, nor are they authorised to give any guarantee or warranty nor make any representation on the Company's part other than those contained in this document.

GUARANTEE AS TO REPAIRS AND OVERALLS

The Guarantee and Conditions set forth above cover, and are applicable to, repairs executed by the Company, with the exception that the period of Guarantee is for three calendar months from the date of completion of repairs.

Cars which are sent for repair will be driven by the Company's employees and/or Agents at the risk and responsibility of the owners only. Repairs of cars are undertaken only on the assumption that the owners give the Company authority to drive the vehicles on their behalf.

This is to Certify that Car number...has this day been registered as the

property of... of..

and is covered by the guarantee above set forth.

Dated..

   For and on behalf of JAGUAR CARS, LTD.,
   FOLESHILL, COVENTRY, ENGLAND. ....

CONVERSION TABLES

METRIC INTO ENGLISH MEASURE

1 millimetre is approximately $\frac{1}{25}''$, and is exactly $\cdot 03937''$.
1 centimetre is approximately $\frac{13}{33}''$, and is exactly $\cdot 3937''$.
1 metre is approximately $39\frac{3}{8}''$, and is exactly $39\cdot 37''$ or $1\cdot 0936$ yards.
1 kilometre is approximately $\frac{5}{8}$ mile, and is exactly $\cdot 6213$ miles.
1 kilogramme is approximately $2\frac{1}{4}$ lbs., and is exactly $2\cdot 21$ lbs.
1 litre is approximately $1\frac{3}{4}$ pints, and is exactly $1\cdot 76$ pints.
To convert metres to yards, multiply by 70 and divide by 64.
To convert kilometres to miles, multiply by 5 and divide by 8 (approx.).
To convert litres to pints, multiply by 88 and divide by 50.
To convert grammes to ounces, multiply by 567 and divide by 20.
To find the cubical contents of a motor cylinder, square the diameter (or bore), multiply by $0\cdot 7854$, and multiply the result by the stroke.
1 M.P.G. = $0\cdot 3546$ kilometres per litre or $3\cdot 84$ litres per kilometre.

MILES INTO KILOMETRES

Kilo.	Miles	Kilo.	Miles	Kilo.	Miles	Kilo.	Miles	Kilo.	Miles
1	$\frac{5}{8}$	16	10	31	$19\frac{1}{4}$	46	$28\frac{5}{8}$	60	$37\frac{1}{4}$
2	$1\frac{1}{4}$	17	$10\frac{5}{8}$	32	$19\frac{7}{8}$	47	$29\frac{1}{4}$	70	$43\frac{1}{2}$
3	$1\frac{7}{8}$	18	$11\frac{1}{4}$	33	$20\frac{1}{2}$	48	$29\frac{7}{8}$	80	$49\frac{3}{4}$
4	$2\frac{1}{2}$	19	$11\frac{3}{4}$	34	$21\frac{1}{8}$	49	$30\frac{1}{2}$	90	$55\frac{7}{8}$
5	$3\frac{1}{8}$	20	$12\frac{3}{8}$	35	$21\frac{3}{4}$	50	$31\frac{1}{8}$	100	$62\frac{1}{8}$
6	$3\frac{3}{4}$	21	13	36	$22\frac{3}{8}$	51	$31\frac{3}{4}$	200	$124\frac{1}{4}$
7	$4\frac{3}{8}$	22	$13\frac{5}{8}$	37	23	52	$32\frac{1}{4}$	300	$186\frac{3}{8}$
8	5	23	$14\frac{1}{4}$	38	$23\frac{5}{8}$	53	$32\frac{7}{8}$	400	$248\frac{1}{2}$
9	$5\frac{5}{8}$	24	$14\frac{7}{8}$	39	$24\frac{1}{4}$	54	$33\frac{1}{2}$	500	$310\frac{3}{4}$
10	$6\frac{1}{4}$	25	$15\frac{1}{2}$	40	$24\frac{7}{8}$	55	$34\frac{1}{8}$	600	$372\frac{7}{8}$
11	$6\frac{7}{8}$	26	$16\frac{1}{8}$	41	$25\frac{1}{2}$	56	$34\frac{3}{4}$	700	435
12	$7\frac{1}{2}$	27	$16\frac{3}{4}$	42	$26\frac{1}{8}$	57	$35\frac{3}{8}$	800	$497\frac{1}{4}$
13	$8\frac{1}{8}$	28	$17\frac{3}{8}$	43	$26\frac{3}{4}$	58	36	900	$559\frac{1}{4}$
14	$8\frac{3}{4}$	29	18	44	$27\frac{3}{8}$	59	$36\frac{5}{8}$	1000	$621\frac{3}{8}$
15	$9\frac{3}{8}$	30	$18\frac{5}{8}$	45	28				

PINTS AND GALLONS TO LITRES

Pints	Gallons	Litres Approx.	Litres Exact	Pints	Gallons	Litres Approx.	Litres Exact
1	$\frac{1}{8}$	$\frac{1}{2}$	$\cdot 57$	40	5	23	22·75
2	$\frac{1}{4}$	1	1·14	48	6	27	27·30
3	$\frac{3}{8}$	$1\frac{1}{2}$	1·71	56	7	32	31·85
4	$\frac{1}{2}$	$2\frac{1}{4}$	2·27	64	8	$36\frac{1}{2}$	36·40
8	1	$4\frac{1}{2}$	4·54	72	9	41	40·95
16	2	9	9·10	80	10	$45\frac{1}{2}$	45·50
24	3	$13\frac{1}{2}$	13·65	88	11	50	50·05
32	4	18	18·20	96	12	$54\frac{1}{2}$	54·60

CONVERSION TABLES

RELATIVE VALUE OF MILLIMETRES AND INCHES

mm.	Inches	mm.	Inches	mm.	Inches	mm.	Inches
1	0·0394	26	1·0236	51	2·0079	76	2·9922
2	0·0787	27	1·0630	52	2·0473	77	3·0315
3	0·1181	28	1·1024	53	2·0866	78	3·0709
4	0·1575	29	1·1417	54	2·1260	79	3·1103
5	0·1968	30	1·1811	55	2·1654	80	3·1496
6	0·2362	31	1·2205	56	2·2047	81	3·1890
7	0·2756	32	1·2598	57	2·2441	82	3·2284
8	0·3150	33	1·2992	58	2·2835	83	3·2677
9	0·3543	34	1·3386	59	2·3228	84	3·3071
10	0·3937	35	1·3780	60	2·3622	85	3·3465
11	0·4331	36	1·4173	61	2·4016	86	3·3859
12	0·4724	37	1·4567	62	2·4410	87	3·4252
13	0·5118	38	1·4961	63	2·4803	88	3·4646
14	0·5512	39	1·5354	64	2·5197	89	3·5040
15	0·5906	40	1·5748	65	2·5591	90	3·5433
16	0·6299	41	1·6142	66	2·5984	91	3·5827
17	0·6693	42	1·6536	67	2·6378	92	3·6221
18	0·7087	43	1·6929	68	2·6772	93	3·6614
19	0·7480	44	1·7323	69	2·7166	94	3·7008
20	0·7874	45	1·7717	70	2·7559	95	3·7402
21	0·8268	46	1·8110	71	2·7953	96	3·7796
22	0·8661	47	1·8504	72	2·8347	97	3·8189
23	0·9055	48	1·8898	73	2·8740	98	3·8583
24	0·9449	49	1·9291	74	2·9134	99	3·8977
25	0·9843	50	1·9685	75	2·9528	100	3·9370

RELATIVE VALUE OF INCHES AND MILLIMETRES

Inches	0	$\frac{1}{16}$	$\frac{1}{8}$	$\frac{3}{16}$	$\frac{1}{4}$	$\frac{5}{16}$	$\frac{3}{8}$	$\frac{7}{16}$
0	0·0	1·6	3·2	4·8	6·4	7·9	9·5	11·1
1	25·4	27·0	28·6	30·2	31·7	33·3	34·9	36·5
2	50·8	52·4	54·0	55·6	57·1	58·7	60·3	61·9
3	76·2	77·8	79·4	81·0	82·5	84·1	85·7	87·3
4	101·6	103·2	104·8	106·4	108·0	109·5	111·1	112·7
5	127·0	128·6	130·2	131·8	133·4	134·9	136·5	138·1
6	152·4	154·0	155·6	157·2	158·8	160·3	161·9	163·5

Inches	$\frac{1}{2}$	$\frac{9}{16}$	$\frac{5}{8}$	$\frac{11}{16}$	$\frac{3}{4}$	$\frac{13}{16}$	$\frac{7}{8}$	$\frac{15}{16}$
0	12·7	14·3	15·9	17·5	19·1	20·6	22·2	23·8
1	38·1	39·7	41·3	42·9	44·4	46·0	47·6	49·2
2	63·5	65·1	66·7	68·3	69·8	71·4	73·0	74·6
3	88·9	90·5	92·1	93·7	95·2	96·8	98·4	100·0
4	114·3	115·9	117·5	119·1	120·7	122·2	123·8	125·4
5	139·7	141·3	142·9	144·5	146·1	147·6	149·2	150·8
6	165·1	166·7	168·3	169·9	171·5	173·0	174·6	176·2

THE

JAGUAR XK 120
DROP HEAD COUPÉ

INSTRUCTIONS FOR OPERATING THE HEAD

JAGUAR CARS LIMITED, COVENTRY, ENGLAND

TELEPHONE: COVENTRY 62677 (P.B.X.)   CABLES: JAGUAR

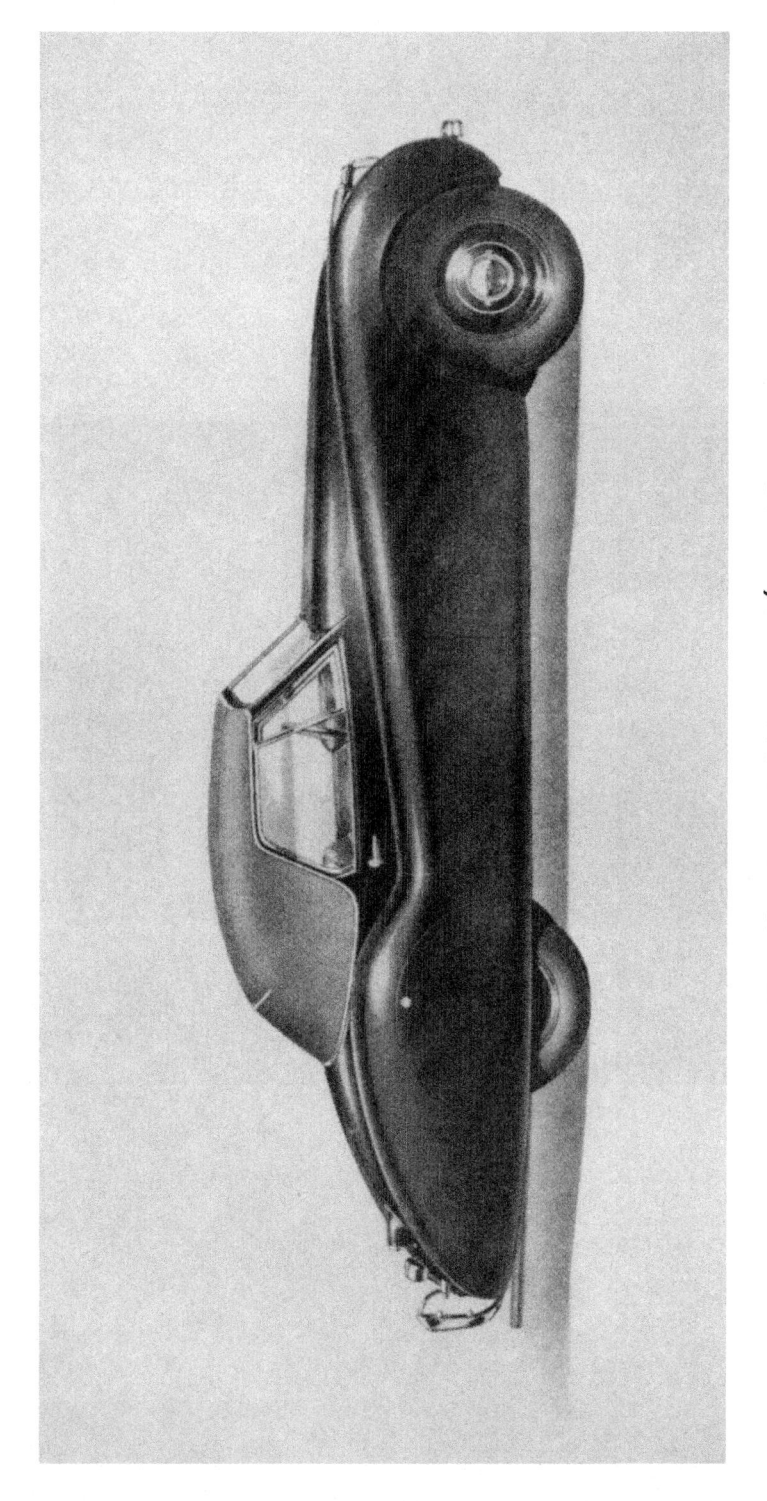

XK 120 DROP HEAD COUPÉ MODEL.

TO LOWER THE HEAD

1. Wind both door windows down fully.

2. Release the three head locks by pulling handles downwards to disengage the locking claws, Fig. 1.

3. Raise the front of the head and push head bodily rearward as shown in Fig. 2 to the position illustrated in Fig. 3. It is IMPORTANT to ensure that the rear ends of the side rails are not allowed to drop down during this operation, or damage to the top cappings of the doors may result.

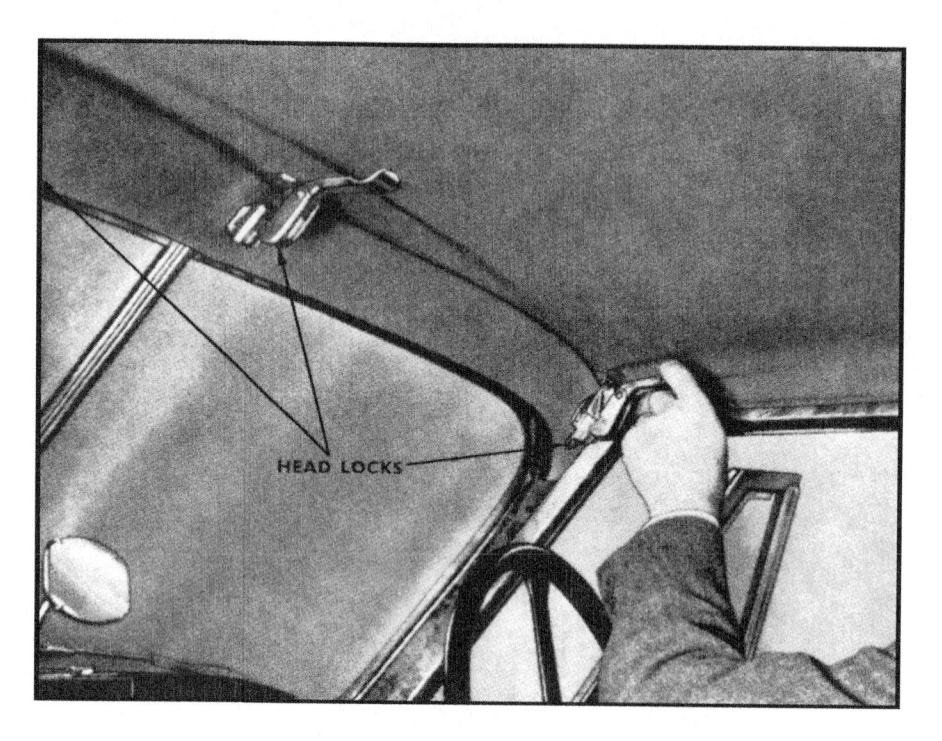

Fig. 1

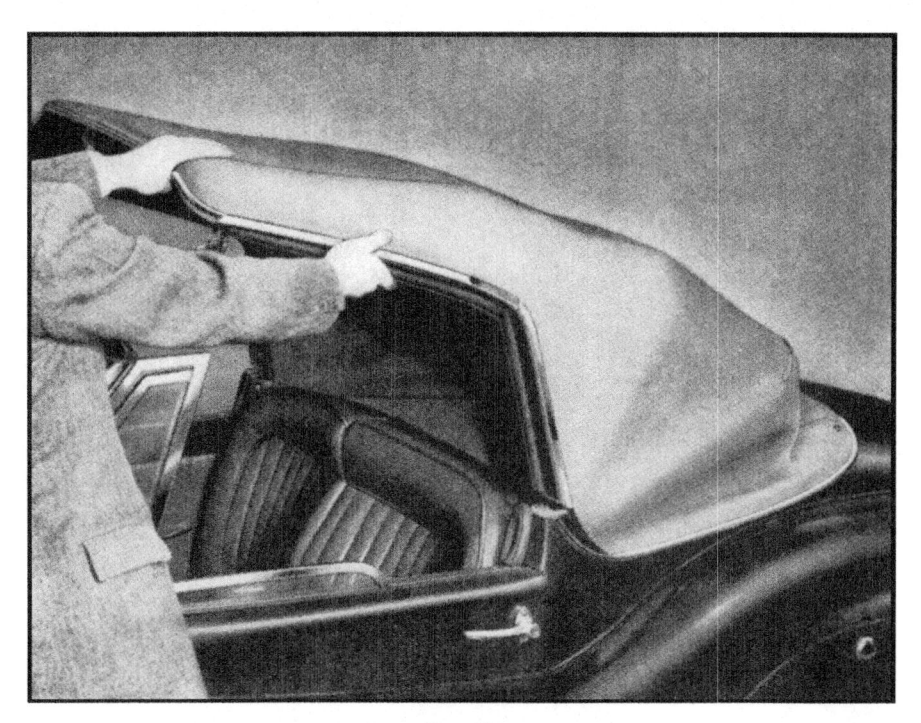

Fig. 2

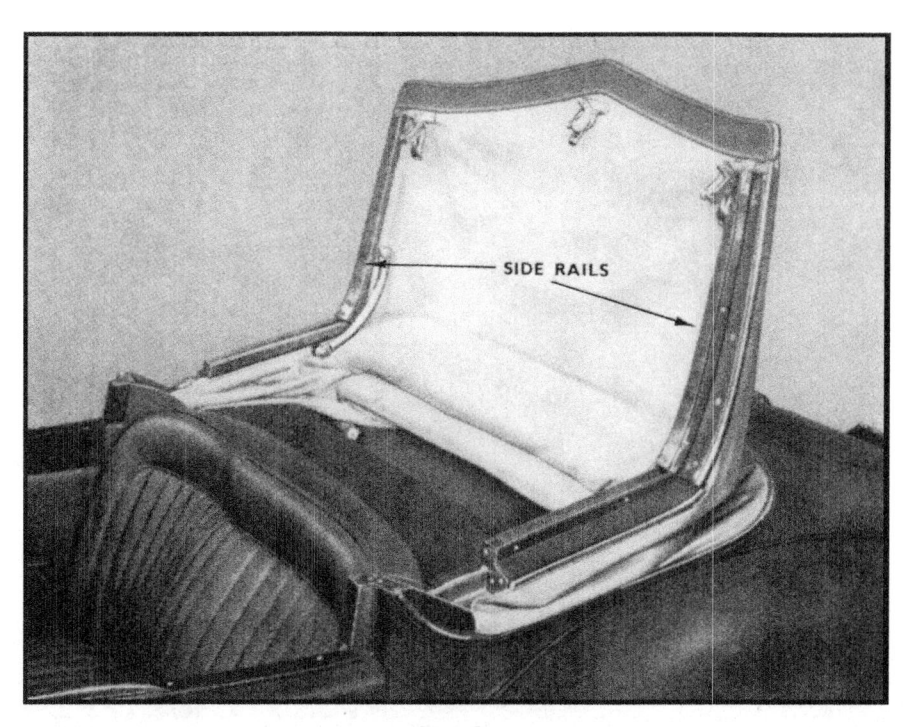

Fig. 3

4. Push bottom ends of the side rails, now in an upright position, forward as shown in Fig. 4. Pull top fold of head material rearwards to ensure that it is not trapped between the folding struts. Fold head to the position shown in Fig. 5.

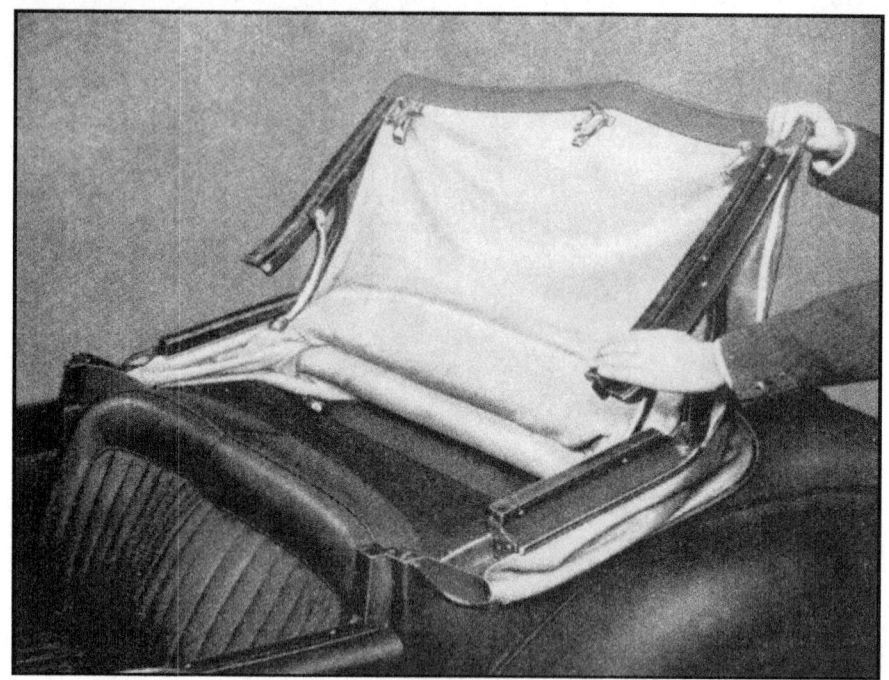

Fig. 4

HEAD SECURING STRAPS

Fig. 5

5. Fold in corners of head material. Insert each of the two webbing straps through the 'D' hole in each corner bracket. Press downwards at rear ends of side rails and secure straps with press fasteners, Fig. 5.

6. Pull all the head locks forward. Fit the envelope by engaging the six metal clips under the chromium-plated beading. Stretch envelope over head and secure with the two press fasteners at each side, Fig. 6.

Fig. 6

TO RAISE THE HEAD

1. Remove head envelope by unfastening the four press studs and releasing metal clips from chromium plated beading.

2. Unfasten press studs and release straps from corner brackets.

3. Raise the side rails of the head as shown in Fig. 4 to the position illustrated in Fig. 3.

4. Pull head forward as shown in Fig. 2 until the front rail is adjacent to the top of the windscreen. It is IMPORTANT to ensure that the rear ends of the side rails are not allowed to drop down during this operation, or damage to the top cappings of the doors may result.

5. Lock head in position by engaging locking claws under catches and pushing handles upwards until they fasten. This operation is most readily effected by sitting in the car and firstly locking the two outer handles simultaneously and finally locking the centre handle.

MAINTENANCE INSTRUCTIONS

1. Never fold the head while the material is damp.
2. Lubricate locks and folding joints sparingly but frequently with engine oil.

Cleaning the Outer Material of Head.

When cleaning the outer material of the head care must be taken not to destroy its waterproof qualities. Cleaning may be carried out with a soft brush and a 'frothy' solution of a neutral soap and water. Stains may be removed by rubbing lightly with a white cloth moistened in carbon tetrachloride or methylated spirit. DO NOT USE PETROL.

Cleaning the Inner Lining.

Dirt may be removed from the inner lining by the use of a vacuum cleaner. Stains may be removed by means of a white cloth moistened with carbon tetrachloride or methylated spirit applied briskly but without pressure.

JAGUAR

OPERATING AND MAINTENANCE INSTRUCTIONS

FOR THE

TRICO WINDSCREEN WASHER

AS FITTED TO THE

MARK VII and XK 120 MODELS

JAGUAR CARS LIMITED, COVENTRY, ENGLAND
TELEPHONE: COVENTRY 62677 (P.B.X.)　　　CABLES: JAGUAR

TRICO WINDSCREEN WASHER

This vacuum-operated windscreen washer comprises a glass water container mounted on the engine side of the scuttle which is connected to jets at the base of the windscreen. Water is delivered to the jets by a vacuum operated pump incorporated in the water container cap. The top pipe of the pump is connected to the inlet manifold via a control button on the instrument panel : the pipe on the side of the pump is connected to the two jets at the base of the windscreen.

OPERATING

The windscreen washer should be used in conjunction with the windscreen wipers to remove foreign matter that settles on the windscreen.

Press the chromium-plated control button fitted to the instrument panel for a few seconds. Release button, when two fine jets of water will strike the windscreen at points one or two inches below the upper edge and in the centre of the arc of wipe provided by the windscreen wiper.

CONTROL BUTTON—Mark VII Model   CONTROL BUTTON—XK 120 Models

In the Summer the washer should be used freely to remove insects before they dry and harden on the screen.

The washer should not be used in sub-zero conditions as obviously the fine jets of water spread over the screen by the blades will tend to freeze up. Do not add radiator anti-freeze solution to the water as this is detrimental to the washer mechanism.

MAINTENANCE

Charging the Water Container. Push the circular plate covering the filler hole in the water container cap to one side. Fill container three-quarters full with clean cold water. Refit cover plate.

Windscreen Washer Solvent. It is recommended that " Trico Windscreen Washer Solvent " No. XAW.30 is used throughout the year. In Summer 1 ounce of the solvent should be added to each charge of water and during extremely cold conditions this should be increased to 2 ounces. The main purpose of the solvent is to improve windscreen wiping performance, particularly in dry weather when insects and other foreign matter settle on the screen, and in Winter weather when the screen becomes spattered with mud thrown up by vehicles.

The solvent is also designed to prevent breakage of the glass jar in sub-zero, conditions, in that it does not permit solid freezing of the liquid in the jar. This obviates the trouble of having to empty the jar in extreme low temperature conditions.

Do **not** add radiator anti-freeze solution to the water as this is detrimental to the washer mechanism.

Cleaning the Jets. Clean one jet at a time only. Unscrew the knurled cap at the end of the jet not more than one turn; do not remove cap completely. Operate the washer to allow the water to flow freely through the jet assembly, thus removing any particles of dirt (with the knurled cap unscrewed obviously it will not squirt).

Tighten knurled cap, finger tight, taking care not to damage the plastic washer. Repeat the operation for the other jet if necessary.

Adjustment of the Jets. The main body and jet assembly is secured to the scuttle with a wing nut at the underside and adjustment in relation to the axis of the car should not be required. The angle at which the jet of water strikes the windscreen can be adjusted by turning the jet which has a tapered thread fitting in the side of the main body assembly. The jets of water should strike the windscreen one or two inches below the upper edge.

OFFICIAL TECHNICAL BOOKS

Brooklands Technical Books has been formed to supply owners, restorers and professional repairers with official factory literature.

Workshop Manuals

Jaguar Service Manual 1946-1948		9781855207844
Jaguar XK 120 140 150 150S & Mk 7, 8 & 9		9781870642279
Jaguar Mk 2 (2.4 3.4 3.8 240 340)	E121/7	9781870642958
Jaguar Mk 10 (3.8 & 4.2) & 420G	E136/2	9781855200814
Jaguar 'S' Type 3.4 & 3.8	E133/3	9781870642095
Jaguar E-Type 3.8 & 4.2 Series 1 & 2	E123/8, E123 B/3 & E156/1	9781855200203
Jaguar E-Type V12 Series 3	E165/3	9781855200012
Jaguar 420	E143/2	9781855201712
Jaguar XJ6 2.8 & 4.2 Series 1		9781855200562
Jaguar XJ6 3.4 & 4.2 Series	E188/4	9781855200302
Jaguar XJ12 Series 1		9781783180417
Jaguar XJ12 Series 2 / DD6 Series 2	E190/4	9781855201408
Jaguar XJ6 & XJ12 Series 3	AKM9006	9781855204010
Jaguar XJ6 OWM (XJ40) 1986-94		9781855207851
Jaguar XJS V12 5.3 & 6.0 Litre	AKM3455	9781855202627
Jaguar XJS 6 Cylinder 3.6 & 4.0 Litre	AKM9063	9781855204638

Parts Catalogues

Jaguar Mk 2 3.4	J20	9781855201569
Jaguar Mk 2 (3.4, 3.8 & 340)	J34	9781855209084
Jaguar Series 3 12 Cyl. Saloons		9781783180592
Jaguar E-Type 3.8	J30	9781869826314
Jaguar E-Type 4.2 Series 1	J37	9781870642118
Jaguar E-Type Series 2	J37 & J38	9781855201705
Jaguar E-Type V12 Series 3 Open 2 Seater	RTC9014	9781869826840
Jaguar XJ6 Series 1		9781855200043
Jaguar XJ6 & Daimler Sovereign Ser. 2	RTC9883CA	9781855200579
Jaguar XJ6 & Daimler Sovereign Ser. 3	RTC9885CF	9781855202771
Jaguar XJ12 Series 2 / DD6 Series 2		9781783180585
Jaguar 2.9 & 3.6 Litre Saloons 1986-89	RTC9893CB	9781855202993
Jaguar XJ-S 3.6 & 5.3 Jan 1987 on	RTC9900CA	9781855204003

Owners Handbooks

Jaguar XK120		9781855200432
Jaguar XK140	E101/2	9781855200401
Jaguar XK150	E111/2	9781855200395
Jaguar Mk 2 (3.4)	E116/10	9781855201682
Jaguar Mk 2 (3.8)	E115/10	9781869826765
Jaguar E-Type (Tuning & prep. for competition)		9781855207905
Jaguar E-Type 3.8 Series 1	E122/7	9781870642927
Jaguar E-Type 4.2 2+2 Series 1	E131/6	9781869826383
Jaguar E-Type 4.2 Series	E154/5	9781869826499
Jaguar E-Type V12 Series 3	E160/2	9781855200029
Jaguar E-Type V12 Series 3 (US)	A181/2	9781855200036

© Content Copyright of Jaguar Land Rover Limited 1948 and
Brooklands Books Limited 1990 and 2018

This book is published by Brooklands Books Limited and based upon text and illustrations protected by copyright and first published in 1948 by Jaguar Land Rover Limited and may not be reproduced transmitted or copied by any means without the prior written permission of Jaguar Land Rover Limited and Brooklands Books Limited.

Brooklands Books Ltd., PO Box 904, Amersham, Bucks, England. HP6 9JA
www.brooklandsbooks.com

ISBN 9781855200432   Ref: JXK120HH   7W4/3065